MW00782655

SCHOLASTIC

Nonfiction Read & Write
Booklets: SCIENCE

BY ALYSE SWEENEY

NEW YORK ● TORONTO ● LONDON ● AUCKLAND ● SYDNEY

MEXICO CITY ● NEW DELHI ● HONG KONG ● BUENOS AIRES

Teaching Resources

Scholastic Inc. grants teachers permission to photocopy the reproducible pages in this book for classroom use. No other part of this publication may be reproduced in whole or in part, or stored in a retrieval system, or transmitted in any form or by any means, electronic, photocopying, recording, or otherwise, without written permission of the publisher. For information regarding permission, write to Scholastic Inc., 557 Broadway, New York, NY 10012-3999.

Written by Alyse Sweeney
Edited by Immacula A. Rhodes
Cover design Maria Lilja
Interior illustrations by Patricia J. Wynne
Interior design by Kathy Massaro

ISBN-13: 978-0-545-22377-5
ISBN-10: 0-545-22377-6

Text and illustrations © 2010 by Scholastic Inc.
Published by Scholastic Inc.
All rights reserved.
Printed in the U.S.A.

1 2 3 4 5 6 7 8 9 10   40   17 16 15 14 13 12 11 10

Contents

Read & Write Booklets

Introduction

During the time I was a Scholastic editor, a large part of my job was finding out from primary-grade teachers what materials would be most useful to them in the classroom. Over the years, second- and third-grade teachers spoke of the growing need for the following:

❋ engaging nonfiction texts that tie in to the curriculum

❋ more opportunities to engage students in meaningful writing (including nonfiction writing)

❋ writing prompts that connect to texts and build higher-order thinking skills

Nonfiction Read & Write Booklets: Science delivers each of these valuable components in an interactive mini-book format. The ten booklets cover key science topics and engage students with lively text, thought-provoking writing prompts, and opportunities to draw. Best of all, when students are finished, they'll have a unique, personalized book to take home and share.

Each booklet is filled with a variety of nonfiction features and structures to help students learn to navigate informational text. They'll learn key concepts not only from reading text, but also from reading charts and diagrams. In addition, each mini-book presents students with opportunities to write informational text. After reading a chart, diagram, or short passage, students are asked to infer, evaluate, apply, analyze, compare, explain, or summarize. As a result, they develop critical thinking skills and gain a deeper understanding of each topic.

Once students have completed their booklets and shared them with their classmates, encourage them to share their work with family members. When children share their writing with others, they gain confidence as writers and become more motivated to write. The repeated readings also help children develop fluency. Moreover, sending the books home provides parents with an opportunity to observe and support their children's literacy development as well as discover what topics they are learning about in school.

With these interactive booklets in hand, children reflect upon what they are reading, think critically, develop their own ideas, and express themselves in writing. *Nonfiction Read & Write Booklets: Science* provides an engaging format for helping students comprehend the features of nonfiction and for satisfying their curiosity about the world around them.

Why Teach Nonfiction?

Research has provided insight into the importance of teaching nonfiction. Here are some key findings:

❋ Informational text helps students build knowledge of the world around them (e.g., Anderson & Guthrie, 1999; Duke & Kays, 1998, as cited in Duke & Bennett-Armistead, 2003). This can potentially deepen students' comprehension of subsequent texts (e.g., Wilson & Anderson, 1986, as cited in Duke & Bennett-Armistead, 2003).

❋ Many students struggle with content area reading (Vacca, 2002; Walpole, 1998, as cited in Kristo and Bamford, 2004). Providing students with high-quality nonfiction materials may better prepare them to meet these challenges.

❋ Studies have shown that some students prefer nonfiction to fiction (Donovan, Smolkin, and Lomax, 2000; Caswell and Duke, 1998, as cited in Boynton and Blevins, 2004). Including more nonfiction materials in your classroom instruction taps into these students' interests and may increase their level of motivation.

❋ Providing students in the lower grades with more exposure to nonfiction may alleviate the decline in achievement often observed in fourth grade (Chall, Jacobs, and Baldwin, 1990; Duke, 2000, as cited in Boynton and Blevins, 2005).

❋ Exposing students in the early grades to informational texts helps improve their skills as readers and writers of informational text when they are older (Papps, 1991; Sanacore, 1991, as cited in Kristo and Bamford, 2004).

Teaching students to read nonfiction will give them real-world skills and prepare them for the materials they'll read outside of school. One study found that the text on the Internet is 96 percent expository (Kamil & Lane, 1998, as cited in Duke & Bennett-Armistead, 2003). Students will encounter informational text not only online but also all around them—it's essential that they have the tools to comprehend it.

How to Use This Book

These booklets can be completed as homework or during class. Before students begin, walk them through each page so that they clearly understand the writing prompts and any challenges in the text, such as charts or diagrams. If students need additional support, guide them as they work on a section of a booklet. You might have students complete a booklet over the course of several days, working on a few pages at a time.

* **Activate Prior Knowledge:** Introduce each booklet with a discussion that activates students' prior knowledge. Ask what they know about the topic, what they think they'll learn when they complete the booklet, and what they would like to learn about the topic.

* **Walk Through the Booklet:** After introducing the booklet and discussing the topic, walk through the pages together to satisfy children's curiosity and to clarify the instructions. Point out the writing and drawing prompts and explain to students that although everyone is starting with the same booklet, they will each have a unique book when they are finished.

* **Read, Write, and Learn!:** Read and discuss the text together, pointing out vocabulary words and raising questions. Then move on to the accompanying writing prompts. Generate possible answers with students. Encourage students to write in complete sentences. Talk about what they learned from a particular section. Were they surprised about something they learned? Do they want to know more about a particular topic or piece of information?

* **Share:** At various points in the bookmaking process, have students share their written responses with their classmates. Draw attention to the similarities and differences in the responses.

* **Extend Learning:** On pages 6–7, you'll find extension activities for the booklets. You can use these with students to reinforce concepts covered in the books and explore a particular topic in more depth.

How to Assemble the Booklets

It works well to assemble the booklets together as a class. You might make one in advance to use as a model when introducing the booklet to students.

Tip: You may want to have students fill in their booklets before stapling them. This way the center pages will lie flat while they write in their responses.

Directions:

1. Carefully remove the perforated pages from the book.

2. Make double-sided copies of each page on standard 8 1/2-by-11-inch paper.

3. Fold each page in half along the solid line.

4. Place the pages in numerical order and staple along the spine.

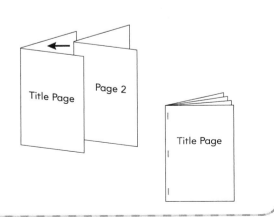

Extension Activities

Creepy Crawly Insects

Ask students to work individually or with partners to create their own Interesting Insects chart, similar to the one on page 5. Students can choose from one to three insects to feature on their chart. After researching their insects and filling in their charts—complete with their own insect drawings—invite students to present their charts to the class. Encourage them also to share any additional information about their insects that they think might interest or intrigue others.

Animal Groups

Have students work with partners or in small groups to label five index cards with animal facts (one fact per card) for each animal group from the booklet: Mammals, reptiles, amphibians, and birds. Then invite students to play concentration with the 20 fact cards. To play, students take turns flipping over two cards, reading the facts out loud, and deciding if the cards name characteristics of the same animal group (such as mammals). If they make a match, students keep the cards. If not, they return the cards facedown to the playing area. On each turn, students get one try to find a match.

Food Chains

Divide students into groups of four. Assign each student in a group a plant or animal that belongs to a particular food chain—such as a plant, caterpillar, small bird, and jaguar in a rainforest food chain. Have students draw their plant or animal on a large sheet of tagboard and label it. Then have the members of each group research their food chain to learn about the different roles and importance of each party in it. Afterward, ask the groups to arrange their drawings in order from producers to consumers to represent the flow of energy in their food chain. Finally, invite each group to use the props to describe their food chain.

Habitats

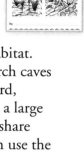

Tell students that a cave habitat is divided into three zones: the entrance zone, the twilight zone, and the dark zone. Ask them to share their thoughts on how these zones might be similar to the zones of an ocean habitat. Then have students work in groups to research caves and learn about the different zones. Afterward, help students organize what they learned on a large chart. Repeat, having students research and share what they learn about the ocean zones. Then use the information on the charts to compare and contrast the two habitats. If desired, expand the activity to include the layers of a rainforest.

Life Cycle of a Flowering Plant

Point out that animals sometimes play a role in spreading seeds to other places. Then ask: What are some other ways that seeds might get spread around? After sharing their ideas, have students work in pairs to research different ways seeds travel. Discuss students' findings, then ask each student to write a first person account of a seed that left its plant to travel to other places. How did it travel? What happened to it along the way? Did it get planted? What kind of plant did it grow into? Did its own seeds leave and travel elsewhere? Encourage students to tell a complete story about their travels and life as a plant. When finished, invite them to illustrate their stories and then share them with the class.

My Healthy Body

What do students do to keep themselves healthy? To answer this question, ask students to record their daily health habits in a journal for a week or two. Encourage them to include ways they take care of their bodies—such as eating nutritious foods, exercising, and resting—as well as things they do to avoid getting or spreading germs. At the end of the recording period, invite students to share some of their journal entries. As they review their health habits, ask them to identify any that they might improve or replace with a more healthful habit. To follow up, you might have students write a pledge to practice healthful habits (or to add new healthful habits to their routines). They can record the pledge in their journal and use it as an inspiration and reminder to be as healthy as they can be.

Sound

Take students on a listening walk. Have them bring along a pencil and several sheets of paper. Before starting out, ask students to draw a line down the middle of a sheet of paper and write the heading "Soft Sounds" on one side and "Loud Sounds" on the other. Have them do the same on another sheet of paper, using the headings "High Pitch" and "Low Pitch." Then, as students walk around the school, have them listen for different sounds. Do they hear loud or soft sounds? Do the sounds have a high or low pitch? Pause occasionally to allow students to write down some of the sound-makers around them, writing each on the page and in the column that best describes the sound it makes. Point out that some sounds might be recorded on both pages. For example, a whistle might go in the columns for "Loud Sounds" and "High Pitch." After returning to the room, invite students to share and compare their charts with the class.

Wild, Windy Weather

List and review some of the weather-related words from the booklet, such as *blizzard, temperature, thunderstorm, wind, tornado, twister, hurricane, rain,* and *landfall.* Afterward, have students use the words to create a mini-dictionary. Instruct them to write each word on a separate half-sheet of paper, record its meaning, use it in a sentence, then add an illustration, if desired. Have them bind their pages in alphabetical order. (They might use a metal binder ring so they can add new pages to their dictionary.) To extend, invite students to create their own word-find and crossword puzzles using the weather words from their dictionary. They can switch puzzles with partners to complete.

Our Home, Earth

Label each of three sheets of chart paper with "In My Home," "In My School," or "In My Community." Then brainstorm with students a list of things that they can do in each place to help make Earth a healthy place to live, such as recycling paper, picking up trash, turning out lights, reusing plastic containers, biking short distances instead of riding in a car, and planting trees. (Some responses might go on all of the charts.) When finished, review and compare the lists. Then divide a length of bulletin board paper into three sections, each labeled with a heading from the charts. Form three groups of students, assign a section of the paper to each one, then have the students draw scenes to depict ways they can take care of Earth in their section. They can use the lists generated earlier for ideas. Display the completed mural in the hallway with the title "Taking Care of Earth."

Our Solar System

Play a guessing game to reinforce students' knowledge about the planets. First, write facts about each planet on separate index cards. You can take facts from the booklet, as well as include other facts that students have shared or discovered in their research. Then form small groups to play the game. To start, give a student one of the fact cards, asking him or her to read it silently and keep the identity of the planet a secret. Then invite others in the group to ask the student *yes* or *no* questions about the mystery planet until they guess its identity.

Selected References

Boynton, A. & Blevins, W. (2005). *Nonfiction passages with graphic organizers for independent practice: Grades 2–4.* New York: Scholastic.

Boynton, A. & Blevins, W. (2004). *Teaching students to read nonfiction: Grades 2–4.* New York: Scholastic.

Duke, N. K. & Bennett-Armistead, S.V. (2003). *Reading & writing informational text in the primary grades.* New York: Scholastic.

Kristo, J. V. & Bamford, R. A. (2004). *Nonfiction in focus.* New York: Scholastic.

Connection to the Standards

These booklets are designed to support you in meeting the following standards outlined by Mid-continent Research for Education and Learning (McREL), an organization that collects and synthesizes national and state standards.

Reading

- Uses reading skills and strategies to understand and interpret informational texts
- Uses meaning clues such captions, title, cover, and headings to aid comprehension and make predictions about content
- Understands the main idea and supporting details in text
- Summarizes information found in text (retells in own words)
- Uses prior knowledge and experience to understand and respond to new information
- Understands structural patterns or organizations in informational texts (chronological, logical, or sequential order; compare-and-contrast; cause-and-effect)
- Uses text organizers (e.g., headings, topic and summary sentences, graphic features, typeface) to determine the main ideas and to locate information in a text

Writing

- Uses the general skills and strategies of the writing process, including drawings, to express thoughts, feelings, and ideas
- Uses grammatical and mechanical conventions in writing
- Uses the stylistic and rhetorical aspects of writing

Science

Life Science

- Knows that plants and animals have features that help them live in different environments
- Knows that plants and animals progress through life cycles of birth, growth and development, reproduction, and death
- Knows that living organisms have distinct structures and body systems that serve specific functions in growth, survival, and reproduction
- Knows that plants and animals have basic needs (e.g., food, water, light, air)
- Knows that living things are found almost everywhere and that distinct environments support the life of different types of plants and animals
- Knows the organization of simple food chains

- Knows that the transfer of energy (e.g., through the consumption of food) is essential to all living organisms
- Knows different ways in which living things can be grouped

Physical Science

- Knows that different objects are made up of many different types of materials
- Knows that the Sun supplies heat and light to Earth
- Knows that sound is produced by vibrating objects
- Knows that the pitch of a sound depends on the frequency of the vibration producing it
- Knows the effects of forces, such as wind, in nature

Earth and Space Sciences

- Knows that weather conditions can change daily
- Knows that air is a substance that surrounds us, takes up space, and moves around us as wind
- Knows that Earth materials consist of solid rocks, soils, liquid water, and the gases of the atmosphere
- Knows that Earth is one of several planets that orbit the Sun
- Knows that astronomical objects in space are massive in size and are separated from one another by vast distances
- Knows that telescopes magnify distant objects in the sky

Health

- Knows basic personal hygiene habits required to maintain health
- Understands the influence of rest, food choices, exercise, and sleep on a person's well-being
- Knows the basic structure and functions of the human body systems
- Understands essential concepts about nutrition and diet

SOURCE: Kendall, J. S., & Marzano, R. J. (2004). *Content knowledge: A compendium of standards and benchmarks for K–12 education.* Aurora, CO: Mid-continent Research for Education and Learning. Online database: http://www.mcrel.org/standards-benchmarks/

Creepy Crawly Insects

by _____

My Insect Picture

Draw an insect and label the legs, body parts, and antennae.

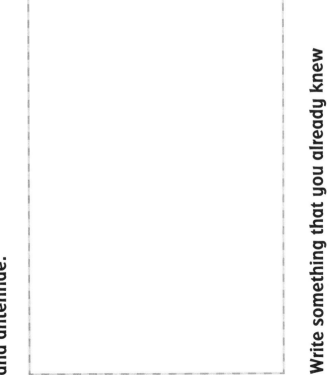

Write something that you already knew about insects.

_____

_____

Write something new that you learned.

_____

_____

What Is an Insect?

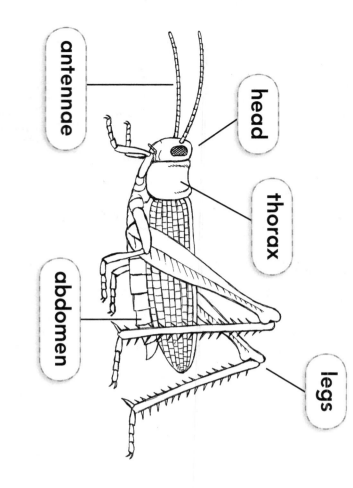

head

thorax

antennae

abdomen

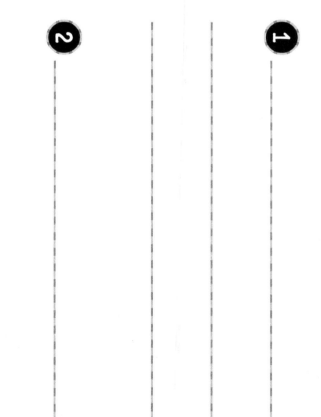

legs

Insects belong to a group of animals called **arthropods**.

What do all insects have in common?

They have six legs and three body parts: a head, thorax, and abdomen. They also have a pair of feelers, called antennae, on their heads. Many insects have wings.

1

Which three insect facts surprised you most? Why?

1

_____

_____

2

_____

_____

3

_____

_____

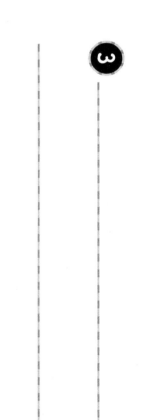

6

Scientists have identified more than one million kinds of insects.

But there may be millions more that we don't even know about!

How many kinds of insects do you know? Draw a few and write their names.

Interesting Insects

Praying Mantis

This insect has strong jaws. It eats grasshoppers, moths, bees, small frogs, lizards, and small birds!

Rhinoceros Beetle

This beetle can carry 350 times its own weight. That would be like you carrying 3 elephants!

Walking Stick

This insect looks like a twig. It even feels like rough bark and has bumps that look like buds or thorns.

Swallowtail Butterfly

This butterfly has a straw-like tongue. It drinks flower nectar, juice from fruit, and liquid from mud puddles.

Madagascar Hissing Cockroach

When this 3-inch-long cockroach feels threatened, it puffs itself up to look bigger. Then it hisses very loudly.

How Big Are Insects?

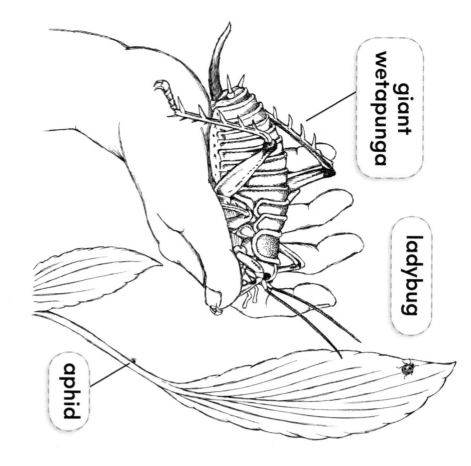

giant wetapunga

ladybug

aphid

Some insects are so small that you need a microscope to see them.

Some are as big as a mouse!

Most insects are no bigger than a pencil eraser.

3

Draw three insects in order of size.

For example: a ladybug, bee, and butterfly.

4

My Animal Pictures

Draw an animal for each group.

Reptile	Mammal

Bird	Amphibian

Write a fact about your favorite animal group.

_____

_____

Animal Groups

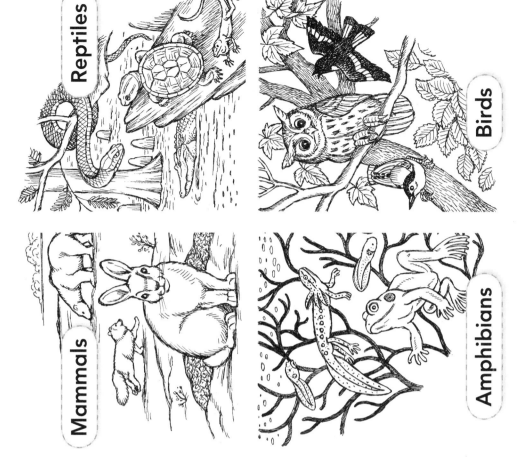

Reptiles

Birds

Mammals

Amphibians

by _____

Mammals

Mammals live on land and in water. They can be found almost everywhere—under the sea, in trees, underground, in caves, and even in the sky. Mammals live in some of the hottest and coldest places on Earth!

Mammals...

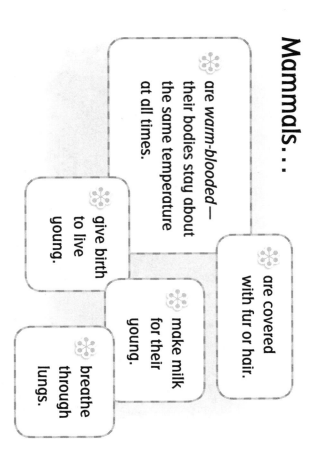

❄ are *warm-blooded*—their bodies stay about the same temperature at all times.

❄ give birth to live young.

❄ are covered with fur or hair.

❄ make milk for their young.

❄ breathe through lungs.

Mammals have larger brains than other animals. Why do you think this is so?

These animals are birds:

penguin

owl

peacock

ostrich

A kiwi is a different kind of bird. It doesn't have wings, and it's covered with hair instead of feathers.

kiwi

A kiwi can't fly away from its enemies. How does it defend itself?

Nonfiction Read & Write Booklets: Science © 2010 by Scholastic Teaching Resources • PAGE **14**

Nonfiction Read & Write Booklets: Science © 2010 by Scholastic Teaching Resources • PAGE **15**

Birds

Birds are warm-blooded animals with two legs, two wings, and bodies covered with feathers. Birds can be found in many shapes, sizes, and colors. Some are as small as bees and others are taller than people!

Birds...

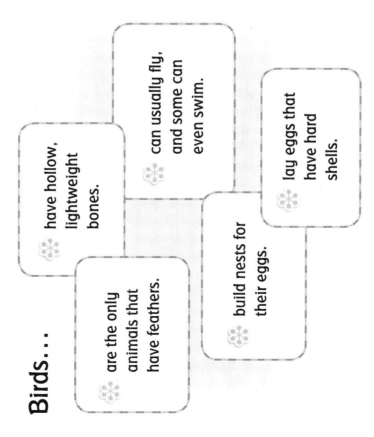

❄ have hollow, lightweight bones.

❄ are the only animals that have feathers.

❄ can usually fly, and some can even swim.

❄ build nests for their eggs.

❄ lay eggs that have hard shells.

Why do you think bird eggs have a hard shell?

_____

_____

5

These animals are mammals:

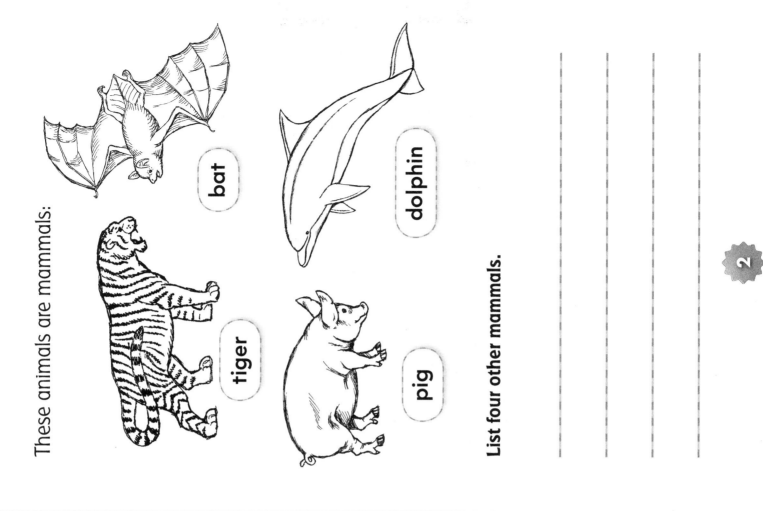

bat

tiger

dolphin

pig

List four other mammals.

_____

_____

_____

_____

2

Reptiles and Amphibians

Animals in these two groups are *cold-blooded*. Their bodies warm up or cool down with the temperature around them.

Reptiles...

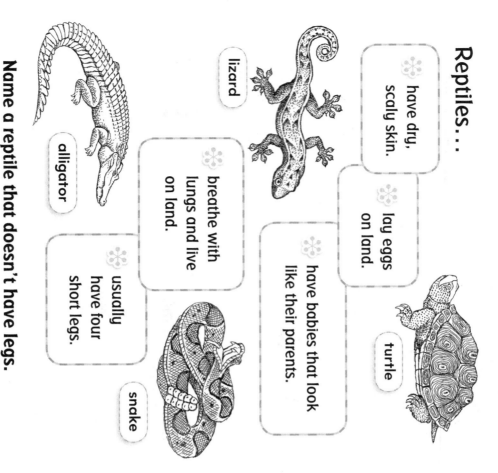

have dry, scaly skin.

lay eggs on land.

have babies that look like their parents.

breathe with lungs and live on land.

usually have four short legs.

lizard

alligator

turtle

snake

Name a reptile that doesn't have legs.

Reptiles and amphibians are also *vertebrates*. They have backbones and skeletons made of bone.

Amphibians...

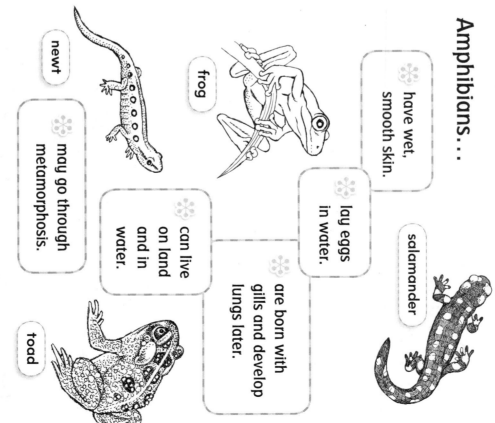

have wet, smooth skin.

lay eggs in water.

are born with gills and develop lungs later.

can live on land and in water.

may go through metamorphosis.

newt

frog

salamander

toad

Name an amphibian that goes through metamorphosis.

Nonfiction Read & Write Booklets: Science © 2010 by Scholastic Teaching Resources • Page 16

There are three kinds of consumers.

Herbivores	Carnivores	Omnivores
 elephant	lion	bear 
Animals that eat only plants	Animals that eat only animals	Animals that eat both plants and animals

What kind of consumer are you? Explain.

_____

_____

List three foods that you consume. Tell if each one comes from a plant or animal.

_____

_____

2

Predators and Prey

Predators are animals that hunt other animals for food. The animals they eat are called **prey**.

A Pond Food Chain

 heron →  bass →  snail → algae

Look at the pond food chain.

Name two predators in the food chain:

_____

_____

Name two animals that are prey:

_____

_____

Which animal in the pond food chain is both predator and prey?

5

The Food Chain

A **food chain** is made up of producers and consumers. It shows how living things are linked by their food sources. Each living thing in the food chain gets energy from food. This energy flows from producers up to consumers.

Look at the desert food chain.

What is at the bottom of the food chain?

_____

What is at the top of the food chain?

_____

Explain how energy passes from the plant to the hawk.

_____

_____

_____

_____

_____

_____

A Desert Food Chain

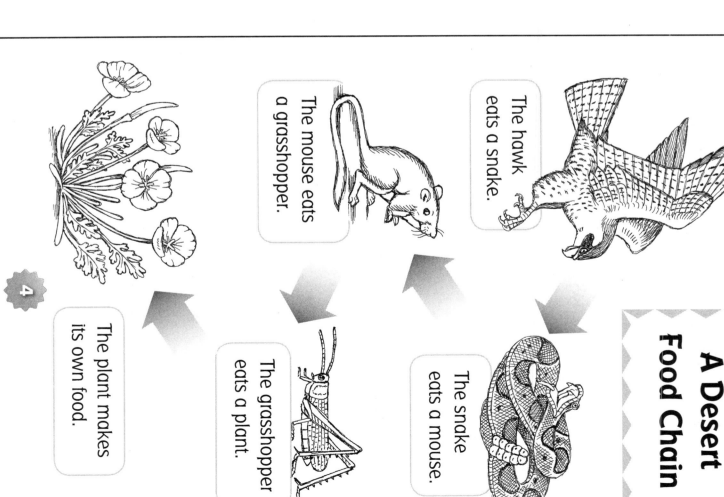

The hawk eats a snake.

The mouse eats a grasshopper.

The snake eats a mouse.

The grasshopper eats a plant.

The plant makes its own food.

Habitats

by _____

My City Habitat

A city is a habitat, too! Draw a city habitat.

Include some of the animals from the word box.

pigeon	spider	squirrel	mouse	ant

Nonfiction Reading & Writing Booklets: Science © 2013 by Scholastic Teaching Resources

A Habitat Is a Home

Every living thing has a **habitat**.

A habitat is a place where plants and animals live together naturally.

These are some habitats:

Forest	Wetland	Cave
Ocean	Mountain	Prairie
Pond	Tundra	Desert
Rainforest	Backyard	Swamp

Choose a habitat. Write one thing that you know about that habitat.

_____

_____

A Rainforest Habitat

Rainforests have four layers. The layers differ in temperature, light, wetness, and life forms that live in them.

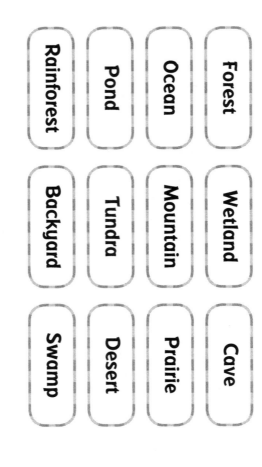
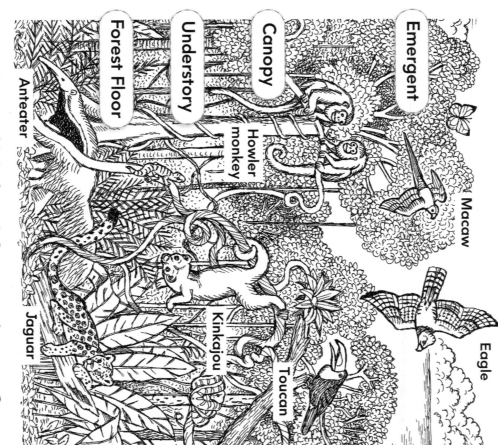

Emergent

Canopy

Understory

Forest Floor

Macaw

Howler monkey

Anteater

Kinkajou

Jaguar

Toucan

Eagle

How do you think the rainforest got its name?

_____

Nonfiction Read & Write Booklets: Science © 2019 by Scholastic Teaching Resources • Page 23

A Cave Habitat

Caves are dark spaces found deep in the ground. Thousands of caves can be found around the world.

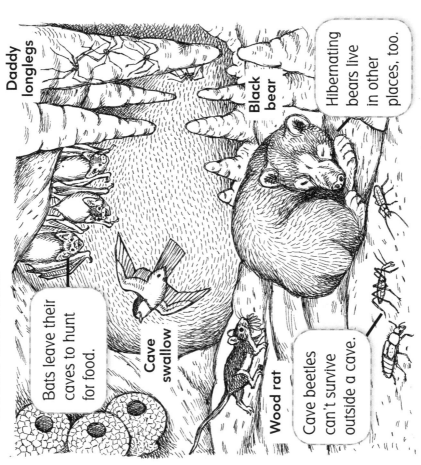

Daddy longlegs

Black bear

Cave swallow

Wood rat

Bats leave their caves to hunt for food.

Cave beetles can't survive outside a cave.

Hibernating bears live in other places, too.

Bats have poor vision. How do you think they find food?

5

A Desert Habitat

A desert is a dry place that gets little rain. Some deserts are very hot during the day and very cold at night. Other deserts are always cold.

Fun Fact
The Sahara Desert is the largest desert in the world.

Many desert animals are small.

Animals get water from their food.

Some animals spend their days in cool burrows.

Why do you think many desert animals look for food at night?

2

An Ocean Habitat

Shorelines, the open sea, and coral reefs are all types of ocean habitats. The waters of an ocean are divided into three zones.

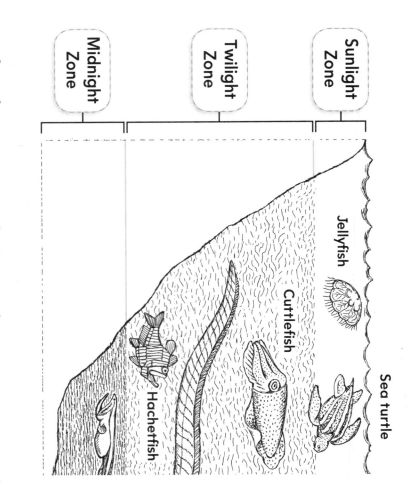

Sunlight Zone

Twilight Zone

Midnight Zone

Jellyfish

Cuttlefish

Hachetfish

Sea turtle

Imagine you are an ocean creature.
What zone would you want to live in? Why?

Millions of kinds of animals live in the ocean. Each zone is home to different animals.

Fun Fact
The ocean is the world's largest habitat! It covers 75% of the earth's surface.

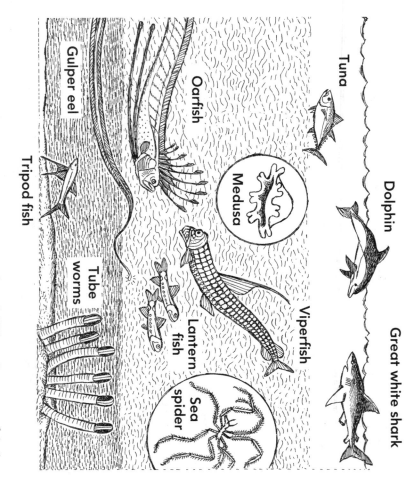

Tuna

Dolphin

Great white shark

Oarfish

Medusa

Viperfish

Gulper eel

Lantern fish

Sea spider

Tripod fish

Tube worms

Many deepwater creatures glow! Why do you think these animals make their own light?

Life Cycle of a Flowering Plant

by

My Seed Picture

Draw and label the parts of a seed.
Use the diagram on page 1 to help you.

Write one fact you learned about the life cycle of a flowering plant.

It's All in the Seed

A plant's life begins with its seed. The seed has everything it needs to grow into a plant. It houses the embryo, or baby plant. It also holds food for the embryo to use as it grows.

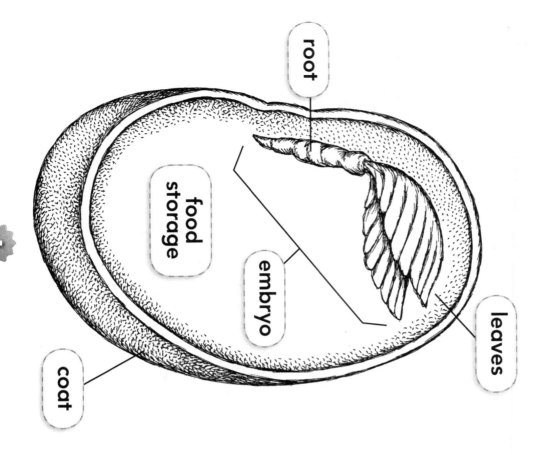

root

food storage

embryo

leaves

coat

1

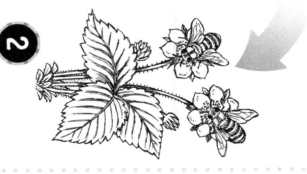

2

Pollen sticks to the insects, which carry it to other flowers.

The pollen fertilizes eggs in other blossoms.

This is called pollination.

How do each of the following help plants grow?

Insects: _____

_____

_____

Animals: _____

_____

_____

6

A coat protects us from the cold. Why do you think seeds have coats?

_____

_____

_____

_____

Why do you think seeds have their own food storage?

_____

_____

_____

_____

Life Cycle of a Flowering Plant

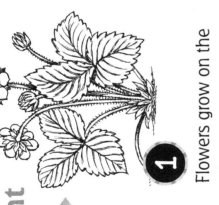

1 Flowers grow on the plant.

The blossoms attract insects.

3 Fruit grows on the plant. Animals eat the fruit and its seeds.

5

5 A new plant grows.

4 Animals spread the seeds through their waste.

From Seed

What happens to a seed after you plant it?

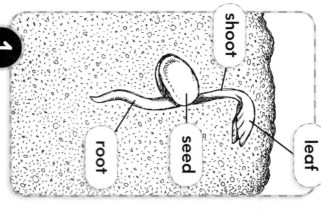

1

shoot
seed
root
leaf

The seed becomes soaked with water.

The embryo breaks though the seed coat.

This is called germination.

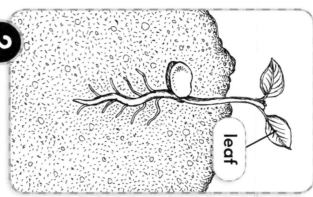

2

leaf

The roots grow deep into the soil.

The shoot breaks through the soil.

Leaves grow from the shoot.

to Plant

Follow the steps to find out!

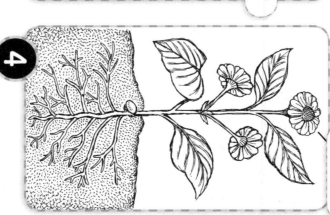

3

stem
bud

The shoot is now a stem.

More leaves grow from the stem.

Buds appear on the plant.

4

blossom

The plant grows taller and stronger.

The buds open into blossoms.

Copyright © 2009 by Scholastic Teaching Resources

3

4

My Healthy Body

by

Stay Healthy!

What have you done to stay healthy today? Draw a picture. Then describe your picture.

7

Yikes! Germs!

Germs are tiny, living things that are all around you. They can make you sick with a stomachache or sore throat. Germs can also cause an infection in an open cut or sore.

---

4 **Exercise and stay active.**
Play ball, run, jump, swim, or ride a bike to make your body strong and healthy.

5 **WASH YOUR HANDS!**
This is one of the best ways to keep germs away. Wash your hands well — and wash them often!

Name one way you can help your body fight germs.

_____

_____

Name some foods that are good for your immune system.

_____

_____

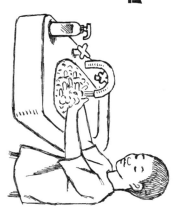

Germs get spread easily.

You can touch something with germs on it. The germs might get on your hands. Then they could enter your body if you touch your nose, mouth, or food.

You can also spread germs if you forget to cover your sneezes or coughs.

How can you help keep germs out of your body?

_____

_____

How can you keep from spreading germs to others?

_____

_____

Boost Your Immune System

Your **immune system** is made of special cells, tissues, and organs. It protects your body from germs.

Ways to Keep Your Immune System Strong

1 Eat healthy foods.
A balanced diet of meat and beans, grains, fruits and vegetables, and dairy foods is good for you!

2 Drink lots of water.
This flushes out germs and gives your body the fluids it needs.

3 Get lots of sleep.
Your body needs to rest so it can fight germs.

Your Body Protects You

The good news is your body has many ways to protect you against germs!

Skin keeps germs from entering your body.

Tears wash germs away from your eyes.

Mucus and **small nose hairs** trap germs in your nose.

Earwax traps germs so they don't enter deep into your ears.

Acid in your stomach kills many germs that get there.

Explain why bandages are important.

3

4

Sound

by _____

My Sound Picture

Draw a picture of something that makes a sound you enjoy hearing. Then describe the sound and tell why you like it.

_____

_____

_____

Copyright Rigby © WPM Bookshelf: Science © 2010 by Saddleback Publishing

Sounds All Around

Sound is all around us. Sound is a kind of energy.

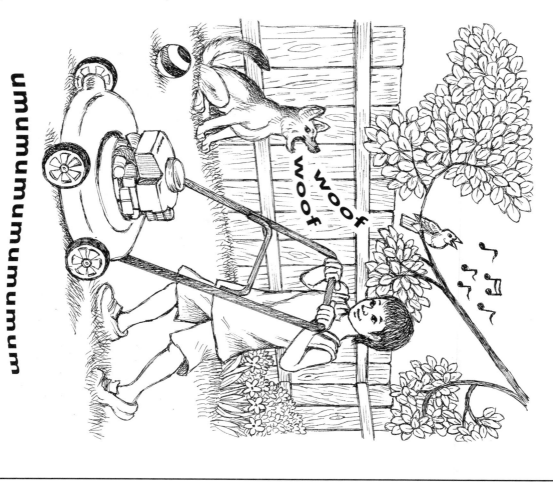

umumumumumumum

1

High Pitch, Low Pitch

Some sounds are high, like a chirping bird or an alarm. Others are low, like a growling bear or a washing machine. These high and low sounds are called pitch.

Things That Have a High Pitch	Things That Have a Low Pitch
whistle	thunder
fire truck	drum

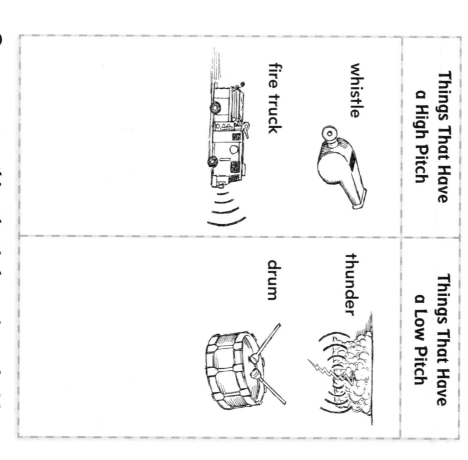

Draw one more thing that belongs in each side of the chart.

6

Sounds are caused by **vibrations**. When something shakes quickly back and forth, it vibrates. You can touch some things to make them vibrate. You can blow air on or through other things to make them vibrate.

Try This!

Tap your fingers on a table. What causes the sound you hear?

_____

_____

Now, blow air through a straw. What causes the sound you hear?

_____

_____

Soft Sounds, Loud Sounds

Sounds can be soft, loud, or in between. The loudness of a sound can be measured by units called decibels. The short way to write decibels is dB.

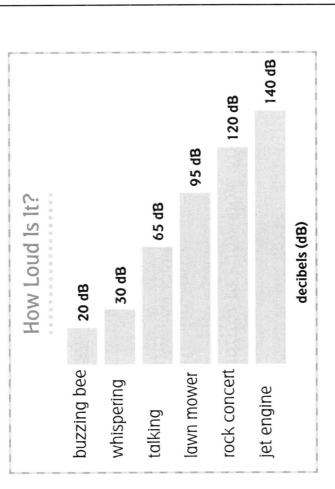

How Loud Is It?

buzzing bee	20 dB
whispering	30 dB
talking	65 dB
lawn mower	95 dB
rock concert	120 dB
jet engine	140 dB

decibels (dB)

Look at the chart. Which item makes the loudest sound?

_____

Which item makes the softest sound?

_____

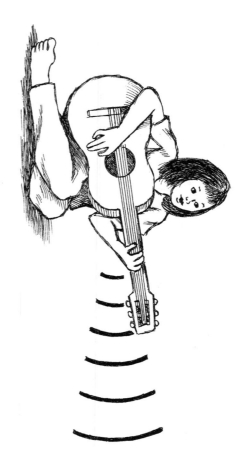

1 The guitar strings vibrate and make a sound.

2 The sound travels through the air in waves.

Explain how sound from the guitar gets started.

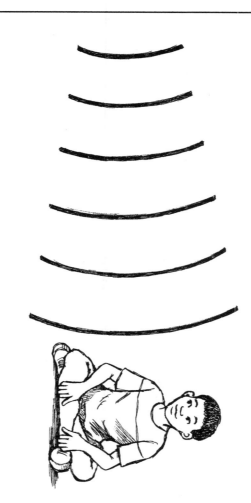

3 Sound waves enter the ear.

The eardrum vibrates and moves three small bones in the ear.

Then nerves tell the brain that a sound was made!

Your eardrum is important to hearing. How do you think your eardrum is like a drum instrument?

Wild, Windy Weather

by _____

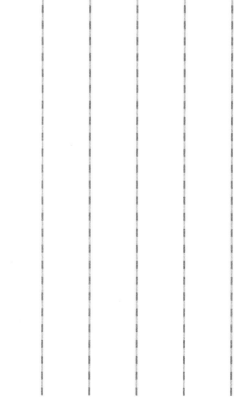

Two Strong Windstorms

How are a tornado and a hurricane alike?

_____

_____

_____

_____

_____

How are they different?

_____

_____

_____

_____

_____

Wind and the Weather

When the wind starts to blow, it can bring interesting and sometimes WILD weather!

The wind can be a small part of some storms. It can be the main force behind other storms. Strong storm winds can cause harm to life and property.

A **dust storm** happens when the wind blows up a wall of dust or sand.

In what kind of place do you think you would see a dust storm?

Hurricanes...

❄ last for days and even weeks.

❄ can cover hundreds of miles.

❄ can produce thunderstorms and tornados.

❄ have wind speeds up to 160 miles per hour.

Why is it easier to prepare for a hurricane than a tornado?

Tornados...

- ❄ form quickly, with little or no warning.

- ❄ usually last only a few minutes.

- ❄ may travel several miles before they die.

- ❄ can have wind speeds over 200 miles per hour.

A tornado can pick up people, cars, and even buildings. Describe what a town that has been hit by a tornado might look like.

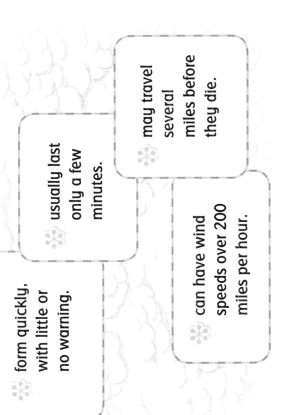

Twisting Tornados

A **tornado** is a strong windstorm that forms and spins over land. It begins as a funnel cloud in a thunderstorm. When the funnel cloud touches the ground, it becomes a tornado.

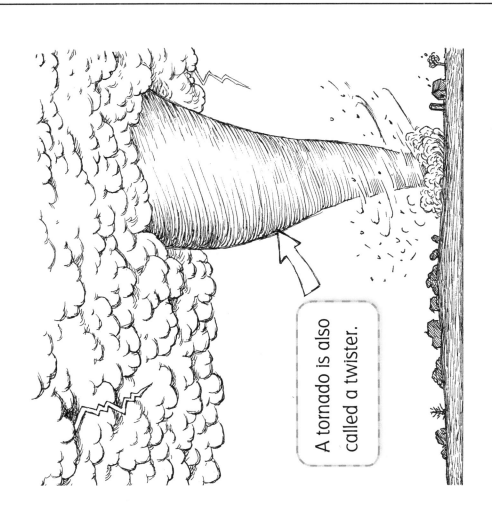

A tornado is also called a twister.

Howling Hurricanes

A **hurricane** is a powerful windstorm that forms over the warm waters of an ocean. The winds in a hurricane circle around and get stronger. When a hurricane makes landfall, it causes huge waves to crash on the shore. It brings dangerous winds and heavy rain.

The eye of a hurricane is calm.

Brrr . . . Blizzards!

A **blizzard** is a strong snowstorm with high winds. It's hard to see more than a few feet in front of you during a blizzard. Very cold temperatures can make these storms even more dangerous.

Name one way you can stay safe during a blizzard.

_____

_____

_____

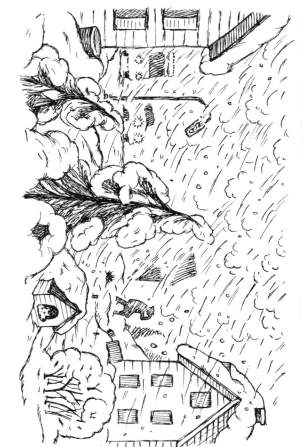

Our Home, Earth

by _____

I Care for Earth

Draw a picture of how you care for Earth.

Then describe your picture.

Nonfiction Read & Write Booklets: Science © 2010 by Scholastic Teaching Resources • Page 7

Our Planet, Our Home

Earth is our home. Many forms of life are found on Earth. People, animals, plants, and millions of tiny living things that we can't even see live here! Life can be found everywhere: In the air, under water, on land, and in the ground.

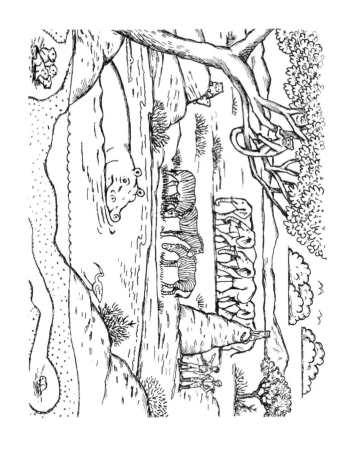

What do you have in common with every other creature around the world?

1

3 Respect nature: Toss your garbage into the trash can.

4 Help save trees by using both sides of a sheet of paper.

5 Recycle as many things as you can.

6

Everything we need and have comes from Earth's natural resources. We use wood for buildings, oil for plastic products, and metal for electrical wires. We breathe air, eat food, and drink water that comes from Earth.

Name some things we use in our homes that come from Earth.

_____

_____

_____

Name some things we wear that come from Earth.

_____

_____

_____

2

Earth Day EVERY Day!

One day a year is not enough to care for Earth. Our home planet needs us to care for it every day of the year! There are lots of ways you can do your part.

1 **Turn off the TV, computer, printer, and lights when you're not using them.**

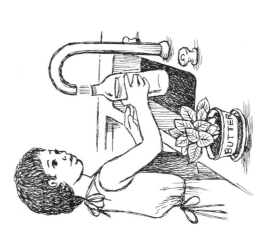

2 **Reuse plastic items like water bottles and food containers.**

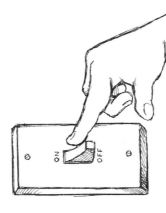

5

Taking Care of Earth

It's important to care for our environment and natural resources. If we want life on Earth to be healthy, then Earth itself must be healthy. Every year, Earth Day is celebrated to help make people aware of ways to take care of our planet.

People share ideas about how to care for the environment.

People plant trees and other plants.

The first Earth Day was held in the United States on April 22, 1970. Twenty years later, more than 140 countries celebrated Earth Day. Today, people around the world celebrate this event each year in many ways.

People take litter walks to pick up trash.

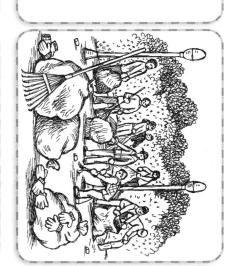

People walk or bike instead of driving their cars.

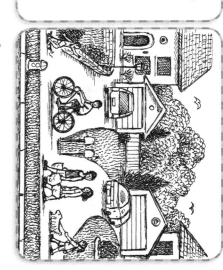

Nonfiction Read & Write Booklets: Science © 2010 by Scholastic Teaching Resources

Nonfiction Read & Write Booklets: Science © 2010 by Scholastic Teaching Resources • PAGE **43**

Our Solar System

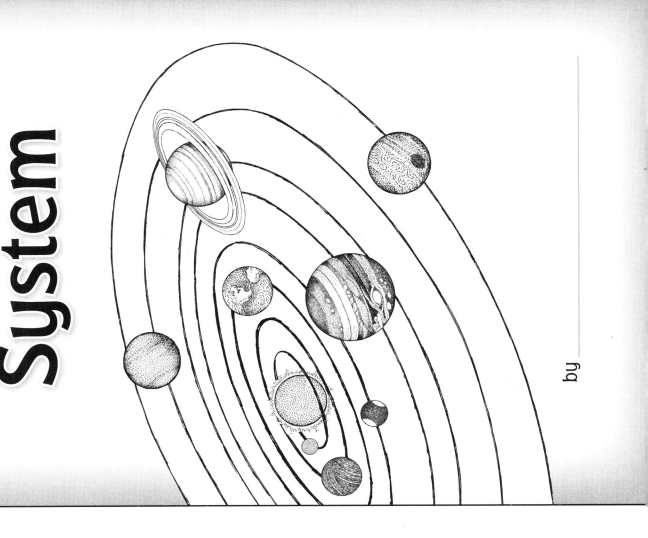

by _____

Watching the Sky

Astronomers are people who study the solar system.

Would you like to be an astronomer? Why or why not?

_____

_____

_____

_____

_____

Center of Our Solar System

A solar system is like a neighborhood in space.

The Sun is the center of our solar system.

Earth and seven other planets travel around the Sun.

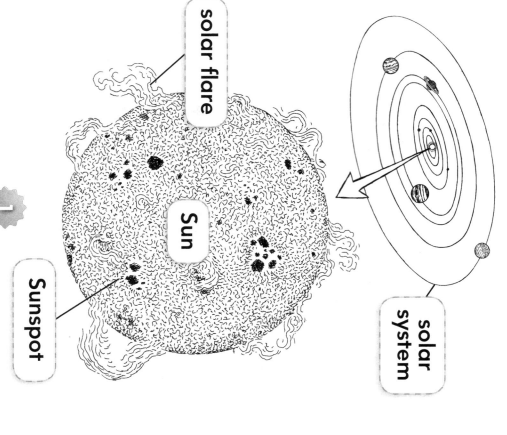

solar system

solar flare

Sun

Sunspot

Nonfiction Mania: The Hidden World © 2012 by Scholastic Teaching Resources. Page...

Gas Giants

Jupiter
Jupiter, the largest planet, is home to a giant hurricane-like storm known as The Great Red Spot.

Saturn
Saturn has 52 moons and weighs less than all the other planets.

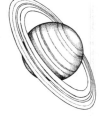

Uranus
The coldest planet, Uranus, spins around the Sun on its side.

Neptune
Storm winds on Neptune blow at much higher speeds than hurricane winds on Earth.

Which planet do you find the most interesting? Why?

_____

_____

_____

The Sun is a big star filled with hot gases. It looks small in the sky, but it is really MUCH bigger than Earth.

If the Sun were the size of a beach ball... then Earth would be the size of a pea.

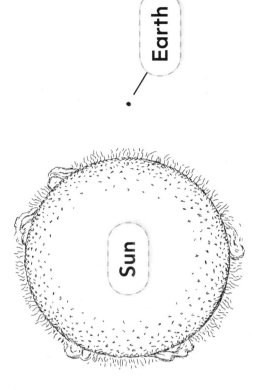

Sun

Earth

Does the size of the Sun surprise you? Why or why not?

_____

_____

_____

Planet Fun Facts

Terrestrial Planets

Mercury
Mercury, the smallest planet, travels around the Sun faster than any other planet.

Venus
A day on Venus, the brightest planet in the solar system, lasts longer than its year.

Earth
Earth is covered with mostly water and is the only planet known to have life on it.

Mars
The largest volcano in the solar system, called Olympus Mons, is found on Mars.

What is something new you learned about planets?

_____

_____

_____

Around and Around They Go

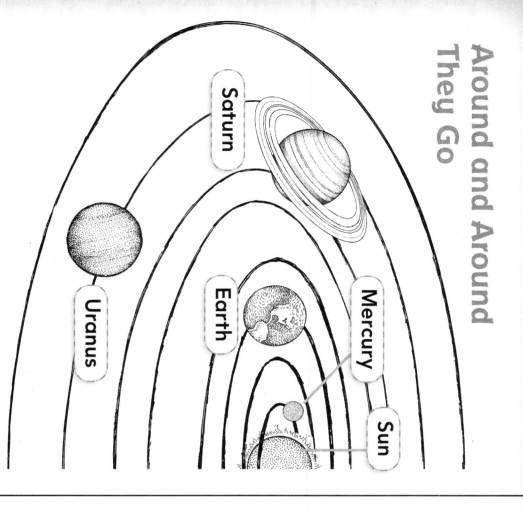

The planets travel around the Sun in a path.
This path is called an **orbit**.

The planets farthest from the Sun are the coldest.

Find Earth's orbit and trace it.

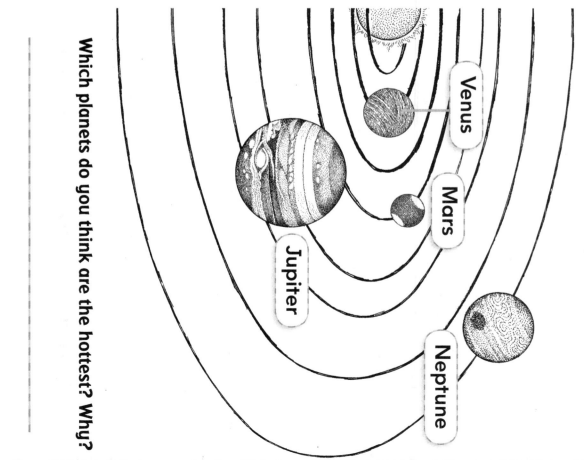

Which planets do you think are the hottest? Why?

_____

_____

_____

MW00782759

Neoclassical Speed Strategies for Guitar

Master Speed Picking for Shred Guitar & Play Fast - The Yng Way!

Neoclassical Speed Strategies for Guitar

Master Speed Picking for Shred Guitar & Play Fast - The Yng Way!

ISBN: 978-1-911267-67-6

Published by **www.fundamental-changes.com**

Copyright © 2017 Christopher A. Brooks

The moral right of this author has been asserted.

All rights reserved. No part of this publication may be reproduced, stored in a retrieval system, or transmitted in any form or by any means, without the prior permission in writing from the publisher.

The publisher is not responsible for websites (or their content) that are not owned by the publisher.

www.fundamental-changes.com

Twitter: **@guitar_joseph**
Over 8500 fans on Facebook: **FundamentalChangesInGuitar**
Facebook: **ChrisBrooksGuitar**
Instagram: **Fundamental Changes**
Instagram: **chrisbr00ks**

For over 250 Free Guitar Lessons with Videos Check Out

www.fundamental-changes.com

Cover Image Copyright: Christopher A. Brooks / Fundamental Changes Ltd.

Other Books from Fundamental Changes

The Complete Guide to Playing Blues Guitar Book One: Rhythm Guitar

The Complete Guide to Playing Blues Guitar Book Two: Melodic Phrasing

The Complete Guide to Playing Blues Guitar Book Three: Beyond Pentatonics

The Complete Guide to Playing Blues Guitar Compilation

The CAGED System and 100 Licks for Blues Guitar

Minor ii V Mastery for Jazz Guitar

Jazz Blues Soloing for Guitar

Guitar Scales in Context

Guitar Chords in Context

The First 100 Chords for Guitar

Jazz Guitar Chord Mastery

Complete Technique for Modern Guitar

Funk Guitar Mastery

The Complete Technique, Theory & Scales Compilation for Guitar

Sight Reading Mastery for Guitar

Rock Guitar Un-CAGED

The Practical Guide to Modern Music Theory for Guitarists

Beginner's Guitar Lessons: The Essential Guide

Chord Tone Soloing for Jazz Guitar

Chord Tone Soloing for Bass Guitar

Voice Leading Jazz Guitar

Guitar Fretboard Fluency

The Circle of Fifths for Guitarists

First Chord Progressions for Guitar

The First 100 Jazz Chords for Guitar

100 Country Licks for Guitar

Pop & Rock Ukulele Strumming

Walking Bass for Jazz and Blues

Guitar Finger Gym

The Melodic Minor Cookbook

The Chicago Blues Guitar Method

Heavy Metal Rhythm Guitar

Heavy Metal Lead Guitar

Progressive Metal Guitar

Heavy Metal Guitar Bible

Exotic Pentatonic Soloing for Guitar

The Complete Jazz Guitar Soloing Compilation

The Jazz Guitar Chords Compilation

Fingerstyle Blues Guitar

The Complete DADGAD Guitar Method

Country Guitar for Beginners

Beginner Lead Guitar Method

The Country Fingerstyle Guitar Method

Beyond Rhythm Guitar

Rock Rhythm Guitar Playing

Fundamental Changes in Jazz Guitar

Contents

Introduction

The incredible and fiery guitar style of Swedish neoclassical shred pioneer Yngwie Malmsteen (born June 30, 1963) turned the guitar world on its head in the early 1980s with a smorgasbord of extended single-string lines, positional and shifting scale patterns, blistering sequences, pedal-point licks and arpeggios. Malmsteen's playing delivered a bombastic baroque/metal hybrid that the styles of Ritchie Blackmore, Uli Jon Roth and Randy Rhoads had hinted at before him but, arguably, the amalgam had never delivered with this kind of unapologetic fury.

When the nimble-fingered Swede relocated to the U.S.A. in the midst of the Los Angeles hair-metal scene, new standards were set almost overnight regarding hard rock styling, technical vocabulary and picking fluidity in the post-Van Halen era. Guitar enthusiasts clamoured to understand what they were hearing and, for a time, assumed that the power behind Malmsteen's high-speed skillset was the result of strict alternate picking in the tradition of Al Di Meola or John McLaughlin. Early method books and transcriptions sometimes compounded the growing mythology, with incorrect fingerings and vague but well-intentioned advice about *starting slow and building it up* to achieve success, but to teenage me in the late 80s and early 90s, there was a nagging feeling that something was amiss.

Malmsteen's use of single string sequences and ostinatos did, of course, display a fantastic and accurate command of alternate picking, but for multi-string picking sequences, it certainly sounded as though there were other forces at work. Learning many of the lines by ear and using primitive methods of slowing music down, it became increasingly evident to me that licks which sounded like they finished on down strokes in Yngwie's playing, ended on upstrokes in mine. The aggression of his ascending sequences, contrasted by the liquid-smooth flow of descending lines, and the seamless integration of sweep-picked arpeggios just didn't fit the alternate picking blueprint somehow. What was it?

Over the years, observations and breakthroughs were made as I progressed from slowing down records, moving to frame-by-frame VHS with a handful of 1990s Japanese instructional tapes, to digital video and the YouTube age. This exploration revealed a fascinating and seemly intuitive system to deliver *all* Yngwie's licks. Where at first it may have seemed like a matter of *one technique for this, another for that*, time revealed Malmsteen connects a tapestry of musical ideas with a set of principles that provide a method of delivery that is so original, consistent, and masterful that it rarely contradicts itself. It offers what I believe is a valid third option in the alternate vs economy picking debate.

The various chapters of this book take the guesswork out of the Malmsteen picking system by breaking it into the three parts that I consider essential for mastery: understanding, development, and application. Part One is all about grasping the why and how of The Yng Way. Part Two is about developing the chops to execute the system through drills and practice routines. Part Three is a virtual lick pack, with practical uses of all the concepts explained, plus a few expansions upon them.

It's been 27 years since I started dissecting this style, and formulating the right method for study has been more akin to a slow-cooker than a hot pan. I've drawn several parallels between learning this system and the study of sports science. I've even consulted some expert therapists to get the terminology right, so please take your time understanding the terms used. Thanks to those whom I called upon for linguistic help!

To my delight, Troy Grady's *Cracking the Code* video series reinforced a lot of what I'd theorised and applied in own my years of playing Yngwie material. Grady has also spearheaded some very useful phraseology on picking mechanics, some of which I've integrated here to establish a level of conformity. Hats off to Troy for great discoveries and trailblazing what I see as new standards in guitar pedagogy.

I'm thrilled that it's once again *cool* to talk about Yngwie's technique, and I'm confident that this book offers an authentic, verifiable and usable method to master the speed systems of a true great of rock guitar!

How To Use This Book

This book has been designed to give you the understanding, developmental tools and real-world experience to perform not only the music contained within it but to help you determine the best and most authentic ways to decipher and execute your favourite Yngwie Malmsteen licks and solos in your study of his vast catalogue of neoclassical rock guitar. Furthermore, I hope that you can take the concepts explained here and use them in your improvisation, regardless of the genres you play.

When practising anything fast, it's imperative that you remain relaxed, take plenty of breaks, and listen to your body when it's time to quit for the day. Remember that unnecessary tension is the enemy of speed. Keep good posture, warm up sufficiently, and avoid using any *No pain, no gain* mentality. The best gains are the ones you can make by playing clean, fluid and precise. Think of it more as *Jujutsu* (from the Japanese *Ju* meaning *pliable* and *Jutsu* meaning *technique*) than weight lifting.

Use Part One to empower your understanding, Part Two to hone your technique and structure a practice regime, and Part Three to apply your new picking powers to practical musical examples. Borrow the licks I've presented, transpose them into other keys and tonalities, and remember that an idea is only as useful as the ways you can apply it.

My philosophy is that speed is a result of efficiency working at maximum potential. Read that sentence again. *Speed is a result of efficiency working at maximum potential.* I'm referring to neural efficiency as much as physical. By increasing your facility through good habits, consistent repetitions and focused execution, you are building and reinforcing the motor skills that make fast passages seem a lot more natural in the long run.

The number of times a skill is correctly executed improves the chances of it being performed correctly again. Always be working on keeping your ratio of clean to sloppy well in favour of clean playing.

Take your time and enjoy the process!

Chris Brooks

Get the Audio

The audio files for this book are available to download for free from **www.fundamental-changes.com.** The link is in the top right-hand corner. Simply select this book title from the drop-down menu and follow the instructions to get the audio.

We recommend that you download the files directly to your computer, not to your tablet, and extract them there before adding them to your media library. You can then put them on your tablet, iPod or burn them to CD. On the download page, there is a help PDF, and we also provide technical support via the contact form.

Get the Video

The download also includes two videos that demonstrate Rotational Picking and Downward Pick Orientation, taken from the Chris Brooks video course, The Yng Way.

Part One: A System of Strengths

There's a piece of advice that I pass on to all who study with me: *Work on your weaknesses, but systemise your strengths*. Seeing both as essential but very different steps is something I believe ties into The Yng Way system discussed in this book.

Working on weaknesses is vital because as players it is crucial not to abandon our musical ideas because of an inability to execute them. We are motivated to break through the barriers because the thought of being able to play the music we like serves as a constant motivation.

Systemising your strengths is a concept that goes even further. Now that you're proficient at an element, how can you exploit that skill or musical device and multiply it into a thousand licks? Often the most powerful concepts you can work on in the practice room are the ones that solve the most problems or adapt to the most applications within your style.

I believe that The Yng Way is a system of strengths as it pertains not only to Malmsteen's style, but also in the way it may provide solutions to *your* challenges. Take the opportunity to make these strategies your own. I've adapted many things within my playing to this system to bypass elements I didn't like about other systems and enjoyed the sonic results as well!

As you work through the various principles, such as picking mechanics, ascending, descending, and "even-notes" strategy, keep in mind that these all form part of a brilliant conceptual tapestry. The challenges you find in various study lines may seem isolated at first, but as you increase your scope, you will see how the parts come together, and how getting better at each element is, in fact, getting better at the system as a complete manifesto for execution.

Chapter One: Biomechanics

I divide the mechanical precepts of The Yng Way into *rested principles* and *active principles*. Rested principles are about setting up your body for the best starting position to execute the material, and active principles are the motions and playing strategies used to create fast and fluent picking lines in the Malmsteen style. These principles aren't restrictions, but a checklist of barrier-breakers for anyone who has struggled with Yngwie's material or is attempting it for the first time.

In the rested principles, we have:

1. *Pick grip*

2. *Pick edge offset*

3. *Picking orientation (including pick slant)*

4. *Picking hand anchoring*

In the active principles, we have motion mechanics and picking strategies. These include:

1. *Rotational picking motion and auxiliary mechanics*

2. *Single-string strategy*

3. *Multi-string even numbers strategy*

4. *Ascending odd numbers strategy*

5. *Descending odd numbers strategy*

Rested Principle One: Pick Grip

Yngwie's pick grip falls into a category that I've dubbed the *D-Grip* because the thumb rests on the side of the index finger and spells out an uppercase letter D. This is by far the most common pick grip, so there's a good chance you're already doing it. Figures 1a and 1b illustrate this grip with and without a pick.

Neither the index finger or the thumb protrudes from each other by more than a few millimetres. The pick is an extension of the point where the fingers come together. Yngwie uses a 1.5mm Delrin 500 pick by Jim Dunlop. I recommend using a pick that doesn't bend, as too much pliancy can drastically increase the time it takes for each pick stroke to leave the string.

The pick is not held by any of the other fingers because that can hurt the flexibility, pick orientation and anchoring that are important for this approach. Thumb tension should be neutral with neither an extreme convex nor concave thumb shape as either can cause fatigue from too much tension. Start with the minimum grip necessary and see if you need to adjust it from there.

Figure 1a:

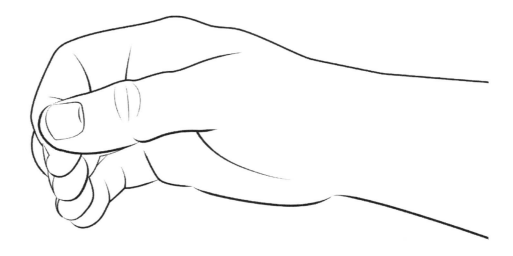

Figure 1b:

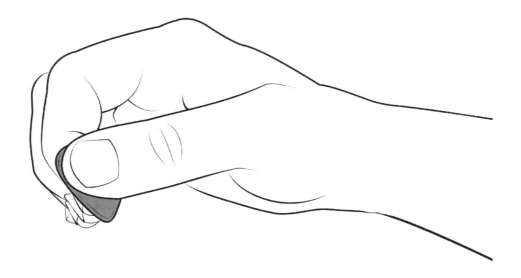

Rested Principle Two: Pick edge Offset

Pick edge Offset is a means of reducing friction by using the edge of the pick to attack the strings rather than the flat surface area. Edge offset is different to *picking orientation* because it happens in a different axis.

When a pick hits the string with no edge offset, it creates the maximum contact and friction between pick and string. It is *on-axis*, as shown in Figure 1c. Doing this can be practical for volume but less efficient for speed.

Figure 1c:

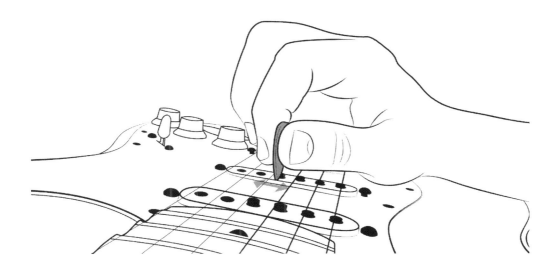

To reduce friction by rotating *off-axis* to the string, keep the pick pointed at the guitar body, then turn it either *clockwise* or *anti-clockwise* until finding your preferred sweet spot. Too much offset will have less volume and definition. For right-handed players, turning the pick clockwise from neutral point means the *outer edge* of the pick will hit the string first on a downstroke, and twisting anti-clockwise from the neutral position means the *inside edge* of the pick will hit the string first. Left-handed players need to do the reverse.

Yngwie leads with the outer edge of the pick on downstrokes, i.e., clockwise offset, while George Benson is an example of a player who uses an anti-clockwise offset, so the inner pick edge leads. Most people's outer or inner edge offset is created by wrist position and fine-tuning from the thumb.

Figure 1d: Clockwise pick edge offset:

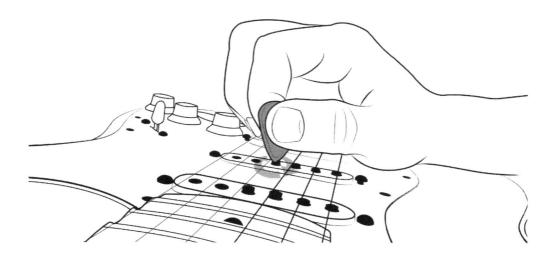

Figure 1e: Anticlockwise pick edge offset:

To get a feel for the difference between on-axis and off-axis pick positioning, take a tremolo picking drill like Example 1a, maintaining on-axis surface area contact with the string at first. Take note of how it feels as you work up to your clean top speed. Depending on the shape and material of your pick, this may even prove difficult if the pick tends to hook onto the string with each pick stroke.

Example 1a:

To adopt Yngwie's approach, a clockwise offset of just 20 to 30 degrees should be enough to minimise friction and maintain note clarity. Repeat the speed test in Example 1a and compare the results. If the pick edge offset hasn't been your default approach, give it some time to become natural through habit, repetition, and combination with the other principles in this book, then make an informed decision on how much offset to apply.

Rested Principle Three: Downward Picking Orientation (DPO)

Yngwie's picking pathways do not occur in parallel to the guitar body, so the study of picking orientation is critical in its effect on your starting position, and on the string-changing strategies in the active principles. In this section, it's essential to acquire an overview of picking orientation and *pick slant* so you can relate that knowledge to subsequent chapters. If these concepts are new to you, they may, in fact, have far-reaching application in your picking style.

The problem with parallel picking motion

When a pick goes up and down on either side of one string in parallel motion to the guitar body, it remains at a constant distance from the guitar as you push it back and forth through the string. Both strings adjacent to the one being played form a kind of boundary for the range of picking motion. In isolation, these conditions don't create any immediate problems, particular with pick edge offset to cut through.

The problem with parallel picking motion is, however, that when *changing* strings, there's a good chance the pick will be stranded on the *wrong side of the fence,* i.e., inaccessible to the string you wish to travel to next.

To see this in action, play two notes slowly on the B string, down and up, with a completely parallel picking motion. At the end of the upstroke, the pick now resides between the B string and the G string, which creates a problem affecting either direction you go from here. If the aim were to play two notes on the G string next, down and up, the pick is now on the wrong side of the G string, forcing an awkward upward semi-circle leap over the G string to get into position (Figure 1f).

If the aim were instead to play two notes on the high E string, the B string itself is now in the way, requiring a downward semi-circle leap (Figure 1g).

Figure 1f:

Figure 1g:

An example like the following could, therefore, become a mess at high speed as the picking pathway switches between parallel lines and semi-circle arcs.

Example 1b:

Replacing circles with lines

Using a pick slant is another way to solve problems using angles. In Principle Two, the issue of friction and therefore latency in one axis was resolved by pick edge offset. In this principle, the objective is to aid string changing in another axis by re-orienting the pick relative to the guitar and following oblique lines of motion. To start, let's reposition the pick.

Treating the string as a *horizontal axis* and the tip of the pick as the *zero point*, moving the back end of the pick down the vertical axis results in a *downward pick slant*. Doing the reverse, i.e., leaning the pick *up* the vertical axis, results in an *upward pick slant*.

Figure 1h:

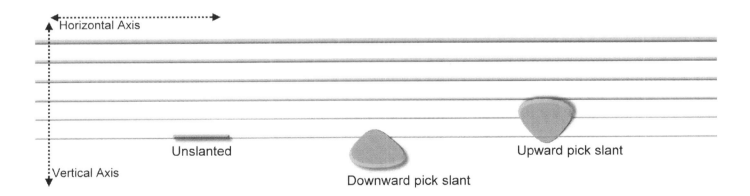

Picking consequently moves in two slanted pathways depending on the pick slant applied. In a downward slant (Figure 1i), downstrokes push through the string towards the guitar and upstrokes pull away. In an upward slant (Figure 1j), the opposite occurs.

Figure 1i:

Figure 1j:

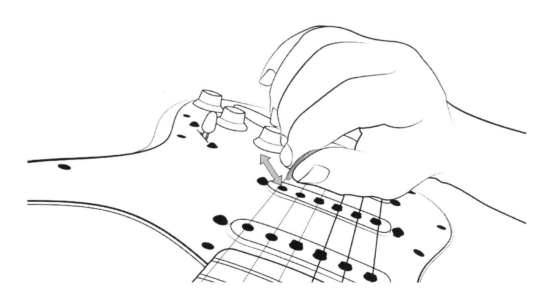

By removing the equidistant nature of the picking pathway in line with the guitar body, the pick will have an unobstructed range of movement unhindered by the obstacles described in the earlier parallel motion problem.

Re-examining Example 1b with this knowledge reveals that the string-changing problem in that situation can be overcome with a downward pick slant. The upstrokes now pull away from the guitar, and the downstrokes push through the string towards the guitar.

Figure 1k illustrates an upstroke on the B string followed by a downstroke on the G string while Figure 1l depicts a change to the E string instead, as per the last two beats of Example 1b.

Figure 1k:

Figure 1l:

In Example 1c, the slanted pathways will enable hassle-free string changing throughout.

Example 1c:

If the last two examples had the reverse picking strokes, up and down on each string, a downward slant would create the same problem as the semi-circle leap. The solution in that scenario is to play with an upward pick slant instead. Choosing the correct slant for each application is important.

Alternating Pick Slant (*Not* part of the Yng Way)

In situations where you find yourself leaving strings on both up and down strokes throughout a lick because of odd numbers of strokes per string, the ability to alternate between pick slants is a highly useful tool to avoid entrapment. Such an approach is a trait inherent to many of the best alternate pickers, which can be considered an alternating or *two-way pick slant*. The aim is to leave each string with the pick slant that avoids the pick getting trapped on the wrong side of each new string in a phrase or scale run.

Example 1d indicates where downward (\ p.s) and upward (/ p.s.) pick slants can alternate to create a clear picking pathway. As you can see, a change in pick slant occurs one note before a string change takes place.

Example 1d:

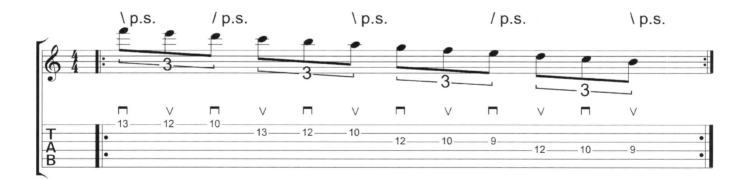

How do you create a pick slant with the picking hand?

In both cases, the rested pick slant is generated by rotation of the forearm muscles, resulting in the picking hand turning either outward or inward. You can achieve a downward slant by using an outward rotation (supination) of the forearm from the neutral position, and an upward slant by using an inward rotation (pronation) of the forearm from the neutral position.

Figure 1m:

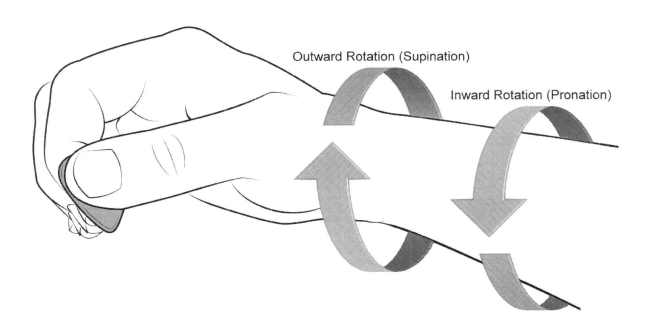

One way to identify a downward or an upward pick slant in your own or someone else's playing is to take note of the fingers, relative to the guitar. With the fingers curled up and fingertips in line as many players do, a player using a downward pick slant will rotate their thumb furthest from the guitar body, and a player using an upward pick slant will rotate their fourth finger furthest from the guitar body with the thumb being the closest.

Differentiating between pick slant and picking orientation

Many players have naturally developed a biased resting position in an upward or downward pick slant pose, meaning the forearm is in *rested supination* or *rested pronation* even before a single pick stroke has occurred. This preferred starting point is what I describe as picking orientation, where the dominant pick slant becomes the new neutral position from which up strokes and down strokes occur. Such is the case in Malmsteen's default picking pose, which exhibits a *downward picking orientation* (DPO).

Picking orientation and pick slant can overlap but need not be mutually exclusive. Many players might prefer one form of orientation, yet still be capable of alternating pick slant when their natural picking orientation doesn't provide the right picking pathway for string changing. For example, both Vinnie Moore and Andy James have visible upward picking orientation (UPO), yet are masters of alternate picking with fluctuating pick slant wherever it is required. James even seems to prefer starting many picking patterns on upstrokes to support his UPO, but still, exhibits a fierce picking style uninhibited by changing pick slant on the fly. By comparison, Paul Gilbert has a visible DPO but demonstrates a use of alternating pick slant in scale sequences where downward pick slant alone might create a trap.

Players who maintain a single picking orientation and pick slant throughout often engineer their string-changing strategies based on that preference. In the genre of *Gypsy Jazz,* for instance, this *Supination Bias* is almost a rule rather than an exception. Yngwie too falls into this asymmetrical category with a picking style that results in unconventional string-changing strategies, scale layout, and melodic choices made depending on whether lines are ascending or descending, as discussed further in the active principles section.

Rested Principle Four: Anchoring

Picking hand anchoring is a precept that results in both functional and aural effects worthy of mention. One of three contact points with the guitar (the others bring at the forearm contour and the pickguard), Yngwie's planted picking hand is a multifunctional stealth tool for stability, string control and muting.

Placed close enough to the edge of the bridge saddles to let notes ring out or mute them, the picking hand gains stability and consistency from an anchored position, can control unwanted noise from unused strings and dictates how open or closed picking passages sound with degrees of *palm muting*. Yngwie is capable of a range of fast, efficient movements with this hand that range from the simplicity of deadening unused strings to the precision of applying varying degrees of muting to strings in play for increased percussive effect, and occasional lifting and muting for riffs and heavier passages.

Developing a range of right-hand effects is a matter of finding a comfortable and functional resting position, then experimenting with various degrees of muting and string control. Movements to try from the anchored position include subtle wrist flexion and extension to mute and unmute, and combinations of wrist deviation and forearm supination to roll palm muting across different groups of strings as required.

Yngwie's fourth finger is often near or around the volume knob on a Stratocaster(TM), especially when playing the treble strings, so feel free to use it as a landmark. The other fingers often meet the pickguard but not in a planted finger approach like that of Michael Angelo Batio.

To get into the approximate position, place the side of the picking hand on the strings as shown in Figure 1n.

Figure 1n:

As you curl up the fingers somewhat, rotate the forearm inwards and turn the pick towards the strings. More of the inside of the hand will naturally become a part of the anchored position. When combining the anchor with pick edge offset and DPO, you should see a resting pose like that of Figure 1o.

Figure 1o:

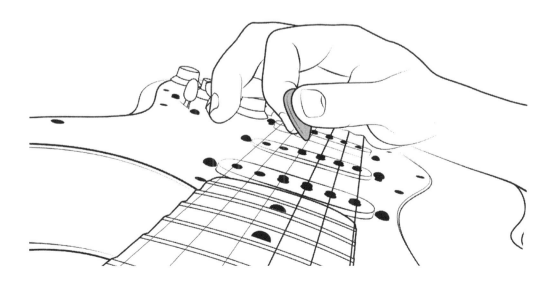

At all times, keep your picking hand relaxed without too much downward pressure since you do not wish to play out of tune by placing undue stress on the bridge. Great anchoring is a result of your hand placement rather than weight.

Note that in the case of single-string Eruption-style tremolo picking, Yngwie floats his picking hand away from the bridge and applies wrist flexion, resulting in a protruding wrist joint more akin to the position used in the Gypsy Jazz picking style.

Active Principle One: Forearm Rotation and Auxiliary Mechanics

Our upper limbs are capable of quite a few movements that can enable and influence the motion mechanics of guitar playing. Some actions can be attributed to one part of the hands or arms, and others to a compound of motions. The degree to which these movements are executed can vary widely from player to player. For one player, one motion might be a core strategy, and for another player, the same motion might be bypassed entirely.

The point of discussion in this principle is how to replicate a trademark mechanical device in Malmsteen's speed system. The dominant mechanic in Yngwie's speed-picking approach is *Forearm rotation*, which is comprised of two components: *active supination* (turning the palm outward) and *active pronation* (turning the palm inward).

That's not to say that other mechanics won't work for speed-picking in general. I could list numerous exceptional players who use different singular or compound motions to create high-velocity picking lines from mechanics like the following:

- *Elbow motion: flexion (bending) and extension (straightening)*

- *Wrist horizontal: radial (sideways inward motion) and ulnar (sideways outward motion)*

- *Wrist vertical: extension (upward motion) and flexion (downward motion)*

- *Thumb and index finger motion: flexion and extension (closing and opening of the interphalangeal and proximal interphalangeal joints respectively)*

We are all likely to use at least a few of these movements in our guitar playing but for The Yng Way, let's focus on rotational motion.

As described earlier, forearm rotation is the combination of two motions, known to physical therapists as active supination and active pronation. Both are widespread mechanics among speed-pickers, but in Yngwie's case, keep in mind that the forearm is already *passively* supinated in its rested position as described in Principle Three. It means there is further supination outward from the starting position on upstrokes, and pronation back inward to the supinated point of origin on down strokes.

The rotation rarely, if ever, pronates to the point where the pick would be in an upward pick slant, so it is a matter of using different degrees of supination from the angle that DPO has already established. Figure 1p illustrates a downstroke having pronated through G string (left) and an upstroke supinating away from the G string (right), ready for the next downstroke.

Figure 1p – Pronation (downstroke), Supination (upstroke):

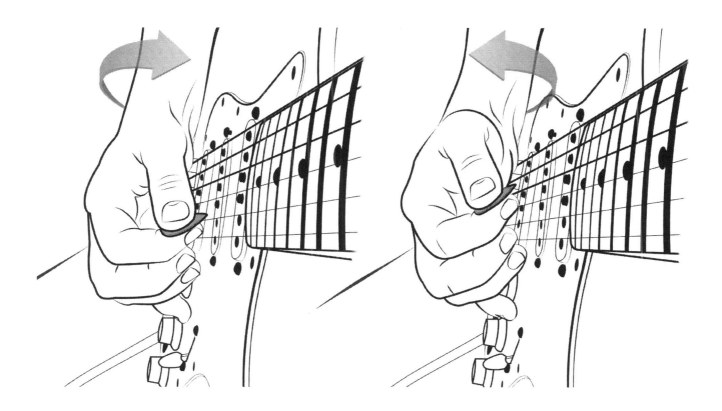

To experiment with supination and pronation in your technique, start on one string with a single note so that you can direct attention to your picking hand. Example 1e provides an example that alternates between 1/8th notes and 1/16th notes. It's important to keep your technique consistent throughout both.

Example 1e:

If your rotation and downward picking orientation are in place, you should be able to perform the string changes in Example 1f without getting the pick stuck on the wrong side of any string. With the larger distance from the E string to the G string, it's natural to use a little more supinated rotation to cover the range. Just be sure that you are not switching techniques or using any upward pick slant in this example.

Example 1f:

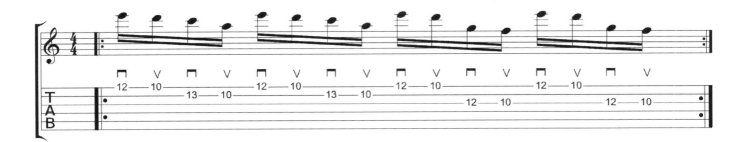

Troubleshooting with Rest Strokes

If you find yourself second-guessing the picking pathways you are creating, another way to line up your pick strokes and double-check your angles is to practice with a *Rest Stroke*. Rest strokes are more commonly associated with sweep picking and in the ascending strategies of this book, but can also be employed for troubleshooting your picking pathways.

A rest stroke develops when the pick leaves a string and simultaneously but silently arrives at the next string in anticipation of the following note. The rest stroke won't make any noise because it is just the point at which the pick has come to a stop.

Going back to Example 1e with the rest stroke in mind, down-pick the first note of the B string with DPO and let the pick come to a standstill at the high E string, which will act as a *guide rail* to make sure you are not scooping the pick up and down with the wrist. Next, play the second note of the B string with an upstroke, keeping the same slanted pathway. You should be able to pick upward as far as you like without hitting the G string. Continue to use the rest stroke for the entire drill to make downward pick orientation habitual.

You can then try the same approach by revising Example 1f, resting the pick on the E string after downstrokes on the B string, and resting on the B string after downstrokes on the G string.

You might find yourself exaggerating the motions at first, which is an entirely acceptable method of becoming acquainted with the technique. In Yngwie's playing, the rotation is almost covert in its speed and range of motion, particularly when combined with picking hand anchoring. This stealth level of refinement will come in due time as you become increasingly fluent and economical.

Anchored versus unanchored rotation

Rotational motion is made possible in both the anchored and unanchored positions by the two bones that run from the wrist joint to the elbow joint. The *radius*, located laterally in the forearm on the same side of the thumb, and the *ulna*, located medially on the opposite side, are responsible for rotating the wrist joint in pronation and supination.

The unanchored rotational motion should be reasonably apparent to the eye as the back of the hand turns side to side in equal amounts between the pronation and supination interchanges. In the anchored position, things will look a little different. The radius can still fulfil its purpose of rotation, but with half of the hand now planted on the guitar, the thumb and index finger will appear to push towards and pull away from the somewhat stationary fingers of the anchor.

It's important not to attribute what you see in Yngwie's anchored picking to an independent *thumb and index finger* motion, which would originate through the flexion and extension of the finger joints only. Focusing attention about four to five inches up from the wrist joint of Yngwie's picking arm reveals that forearm rotation is still occurring, but with less visual clues given by the stationary fingers of the picking hand.

Auxiliary effects of anchored rotation

Auxiliary mechanics is the label I've given to motions that work together with, or result from the primary mechanic of forearm rotation. These are more likely to be resultant movements in your playing rather than aspects that require a significant portion of your thinking process.

The thumb and index finger motion that *does* occur in Yngwie's playing is perhaps best thought of as *fine-tuning*. Where some movement is altered in the process of anchored picking, the thumb and index finger both add some extra range of motion that I suspect is highly intuitive rather than conceptualised. This fine-tuning process also occurs in pick edge offset, flattening out for big notes where more volume or aggressive attack is required, and reverting to slicing mode for sweeps and fluid lines. To that end, even small traces of wrist flexion and extension can have been observed for certain phrases where a lot of attack on slower passages is required. Interestingly, Malmsteen's Blues playing features a lot more instances of these auxiliary mechanics than faster consistent passages.

If you've chosen to adopt the forearm rotation mechanic that dominates Yngwie's speed-picking, use the development drills in this book to hone that technique first and foremost, and observe any auxiliary mechanics that occur in your playing, evaluating their usefulness and either keeping or correcting them as required. As vain as it may sound, practice done in front of a mirror can be beneficial in self-evaluation!

Watch the Video!

To get a bird's eye view of rotational motion and downward picking orientation at various speeds, take a look at the video example included in our download for this book, which is from my video course The Yng Way. Details are in the "Get the Audio" section on Page 9.

Active Principle Two: Single-String Alternate Picking

In the 1960s and '70s, one way that a rock guitarist could add some flash and excitement to their solos was to take short phrases and repeat them several times, no doubt a nod to the blues that influenced so many rock players of the day. Often these phrases were done in box patterns like the Pentatonic scale, so it was common to hear three-note and four-note repetitions like that of Example 1g in the solos of influential rock players like Eric Clapton and Jimmy Page.

Example 1g

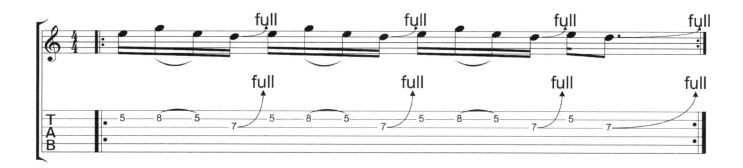

When Edward Van Halen emerged in the late '70s, things certainly opened up on a technical level as a new wave of guitar hysteria began, but Van Halen's solos still contained a lot of repetition-based licks formed around two-handed tapping (Example 1h) and tremolo picking (Example 1i).

Example 1h:

Example 1i:

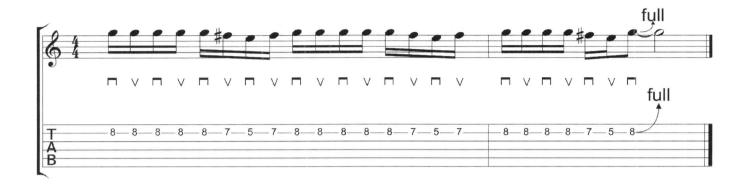

Inspired as much by Italian violinist Niccolo Paganini's (1782-1840) *24 Caprices* as Deep Purple's *Fireball*, a young Malmsteen set out to circumvent the rock clichés of the day by developing a more linear approach to speed licks and tonal sequencing which would become just one of the tricks in his magic bag. This method involves first knowing the major and minor scales up and down single strings. Example 1j contains an A minor scale in one octave on the high E string.

Example 1j:

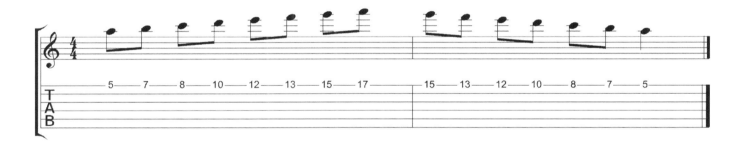

Yngwie applies a variety of sequences and position shifts to one-string scales to emulate his Italian hero, as well as recall the inverted (upper) pedal-point melodies of another significant influence, Johann Sebastian Bach (1685-1750). Malmsteen's single-string repertoire typically uses motifs consisting of three diatonic notes in each position before shifting upward or downward, executed with alternate picking.

A tonal sequence is when a motif is repeated in a higher or lower pitch, where the subsequent repetitions are diatonic transpositions of the original idea, like Example 1k which is comprised of four notes descending from each degree of the A minor scale.

Example 1k:

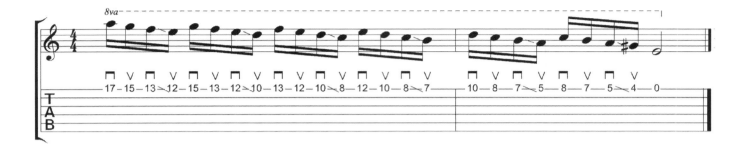

Inverted pedal-point is a device in which the highest note of the phrase is repeated between notes of a moving line. This Bach-style example in A minor is a trademark lick in the Malmsteen catalogue.

Example 1l:

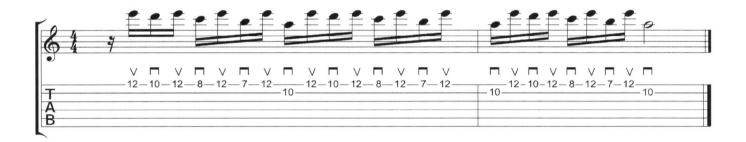

Yngwie combines elements of pedal-point and sequence along a string as shown in Example 1m, which emulates something the right hand of a harpsichordist might play in a Bach Concerto.

Example 1m:

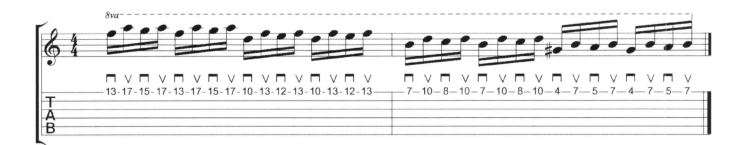

Based on the frequent use of three notes per position, I use a numbering system to explain the melodic order of the sequences according to the lowest note, middle note and highest of the three. So, a sequence like Example 1n is described as 3-1-2-3 and means the highest note of the position is played, followed by the lowest, the middle, and back to the highest. This form is widespread in Yngwie's work.

Example 1n:

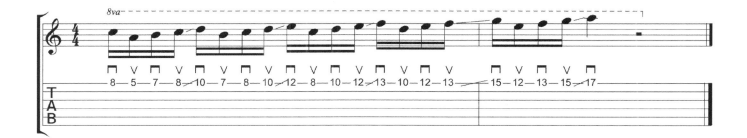

When trying these examples, remember to use the rotational motion and downward picking orientation to push towards the string and pull away from it. For shifting patterns, make sure each unit moves in perfect synchronisation with your downstrokes and the beats of your metronome.

Active Principle Three: Multi-string Even Numbers Strategy

Even numbers are a downwardly-oriented, alternate picker's dream! DPO sets up any multi-string, even-numbered picking sequence to start each string on a downstroke, exit on an upstroke, and have a clean path for changing strings in any direction without changes to pick slant. Regardless of musical style, licks based on multiples of two notes per string will give you this string-changing freedom throughout, as shown in the fusion-style A Dorian lick in Example 1o and the E Phrygian Dominant tonality of Example 1p.

Example 1o:

Example 1p:

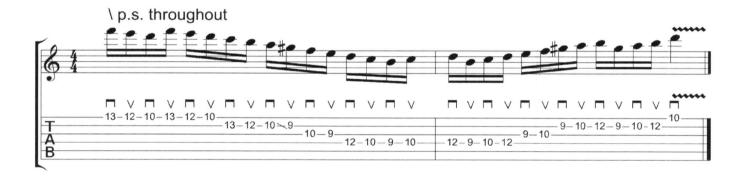

The string-changing simplicity and consistency of these patterns mean that whether each string has two, four, six or twenty notes, the picking pathway between strings need not be more complicated than a pentatonic box pattern, for example. Yngwie uses this to good effect in several of his trademark scale runs. If you remove the downward picking orientation from this category of picking licks, string changing once again becomes cumbersome. To avoid such problems, start *Evens* sequences on a downstroke and maintain DPO throughout.

Even patterns that lead with upstrokes do not naturally occur in Yngwie's playing, but if encountered in other styles and playing situations, it's important that you flip the picking orientation so that upstroke-leading is preceded by an upward pick slant. Example 1q demonstrates this with an upward pick slant on beat 2 setting up the up-driven portions of the lick before returning to a downward pick slant during the 2nd beat of bar two.

Example 1q:

Active Principle Four: Ascending Odd Numbers Strategy

At this point, you should be comfortable with alternate-picking single-string licks, and multi-string even-numbered sequences while maintaining a downward picking orientation throughout. Active principles four and five cover how Yngwie deals with odd numbers of notes, which play a big part in how the rest of the material in this book is played.

Alternate picking for odd numbers of notes per string is not a feature of The Yng Way, but it's vital to have an overview of how alternate picking is affected by odd numbers to appreciate the benefits and consistency of Yngwie's solution.

Strict alternate picking for odd numbers creates two picking pathways known as *Outside Picking* and *Inside Picking*. These terms refer to the pick travelling around the strings or directly between them. In Example 1r, the picking pathway from the G string to the B string is an outside picking stroke, and the path from the B string to the E string is an inside picking stroke. Here, the ascending *outside strokes* are best approached with an upward pick slant, and ascending *inside strokes* are best approached with a downward pick slant.

Example 1r:

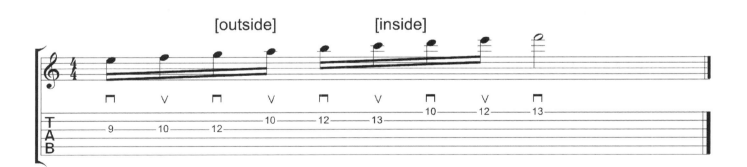

One of the pitfalls of alternate picking is that adding or removing notes from a phrase can alter where the inside and outside picking pathways occur. Example 1s starts with three new notes on the D string and follows with the notes of the previous example. As a result, a complete reversal of the prior segment of the phrase occurs, with pick strokes, pick slant, and picking pathways flipped to their opposites.

Example 1s:

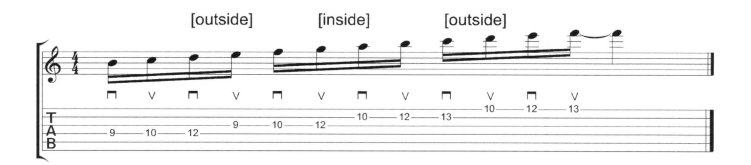

Yngwie's system, however, is built on facilitating an uninterrupted and consistent approach to each ascending string change instead of the symmetrical and oft-changing requirements of alternate picking. It preserves his preference for starting strings on downstrokes as described in the "Evens" approach.

When ascending with odd numbers, Yngwie will use a sweep or economy motion with DPO to turn the last downstroke of one string into the first downstroke of the next string. It's applying the scientific principle of *Inertia,* i.e., the tendency for an object to remain in its present state of motion until otherwise affected. Such a propensity is particularly the case with the improved velocity of outer pick edge offset, as the pick glides smoothly from one string to the next. Put simply, in Yngwie's system, the easiest way to overcome a string change is to push right through it! This directional process of changing strings with sweep-picking is known as *Economy Picking*, but Yngwie is strictly a one-way economy picker, ascending only.

Applying this approach to lines like Examples 1q and 1r demonstrates that with The Yng Way, extending a phrase need not reverse its mechanics. In Example 1t, the notes of the two previous examples are reprised but retooled with the Yngwie picking system, which remains in downward picking orientation and handles each string change the same as the next. In other words, two licks – one approach.

Example 1t:

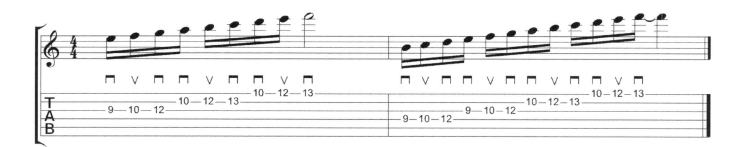

Bass players have tapped into the strengths of this Newtonian approach to string changing since the advent of upright bass fingerstyle, but in the opposite direction from higher strings to lower strings. Using a *drag method* whenever an opportunity to descend strings with the same finger presented itself, bassists continued this practice through the birth of electric bass in rock, blues, funk and jazz styles.

Back in the plectrum-using world, the asymmetrical ascending string-changing strategy has been a staple of the Gypsy Jazz genre possibly since its inception, as generational teaching methods saw it evolve into somewhat of an unspoken mechanical standard, albeit without the pick edge offset or picking hand anchoring seen in Yngwie's system.

It's imperative when developing your economy picking mechanics that you sweep as one flowing motion between strings rather than use two separate pick strokes. Develop your rest stroke technique so that exit downstrokes from the lower strings land on the following higher string without the need for a double movement. The first note of each higher string will, therefore, be created by the pick *leaving* the string rather than landing on it, as it will already be in-position from the sweep.

Watch the Video

You can see a video example of the ascending strategy at full speed and in slow motion by grabbing the download files for this book. See "Get the Audio" on Page 9 for details.

Active Principle Five: Descending Odd Numbers Strategy

Yngwie's second solution to odd numbers of notes per string is a strategy I describe with the portmanteau *Pick-gato*, combining the terms *picking* and *legato*. Legato means *tied together,* i.e., *smooth* in musical terms. For guitarists, however, it is often described as a playing technique due to the use of hammering on and pulling off notes with the fretting hand to contrast the usually stronger attack of picking.

A two-way economy picker like Frank Gambale descends by inverting his ascending approach with economy-picked string changes and an *upward* pick slant. Yngwie, being Yngwie, defiantly maintains his DPO throughout descending lines and tackles the asymmetry of his style another way.

Just like in the even numbers strategy, Yngwie uses the strengths of alternate picking to start strings with downstrokes and leave on upstrokes without forcing changes to pick orientation and picking pathway. A fretting hand pull-off is then used to execute the final odd note of any applicable string. Therefore, three notes are played *down, up, pull-off*. Five notes are played *down, up, down, up, pull-off* and so on. Example 1u is a quintessential Yngwie-style phrase with the descending Pick-gato strategy

Example 1u:

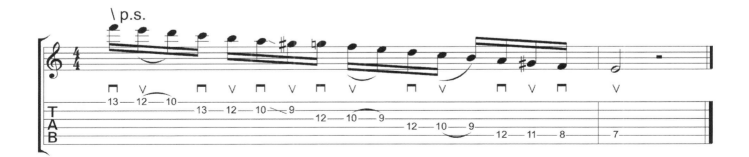

An economy picker would use a different approach to the same notes, using an upward pick slant through and using upward sweeps as shown in Example 1v.

Example 1v:

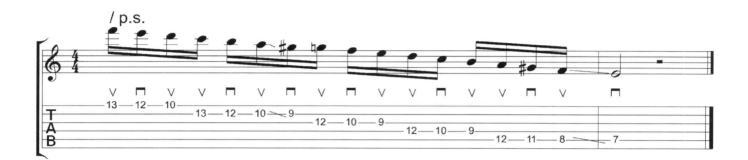

The strategy used in the former example is a cornerstone of Yngwie's fluid descending lines. The Pick-gato approach avoids inside picking, is optimised for DPO, and creates a synergy between combined even and odd numbers within a sequence, since the first pick stroke on each string is still a downstroke, and the last remains an upstroke. The strategic placement of pull-offs handles what would otherwise be a break in the even numbers strategy.

The Lone Note Exception

There is one quasi-exception to the downstroke starting-note template. I use the prefix quasi- because, despite its apparent deviation from the rules, this anomaly has a consistency to its usage.

When a single pick stroke on one string occurs before any number of notes on a lower string, the single picked note is played with an upstroke before the lower string begins on a downstroke. Handling a *lone note* in this way preserves consistency in the system amongst the remainder of the lick by treating it as an *exit note,* as though it were the last of several notes played on the higher string. The pick *leaves* the higher string on an upstroke, starts the lower string on a downstroke, and still avoids inside picking and alternating pick slant.

Example 1w is typical of the way Yngwie begins a legato phrase on one string before picking on lower strings. Even though there would be plenty of time to get to get the pick from the E string to the B string if both began on downstrokes, using the lone note upstroke removes an avoidable semi-circle leap to the B string.

Example 1w:

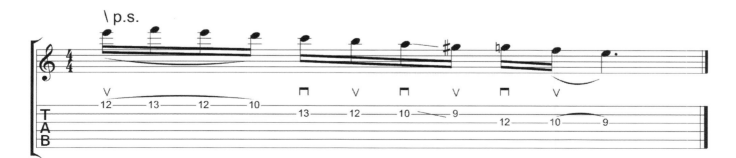

Example 1x demonstrates a direct path from the E string to the B string using the lone note exception. To reinforce how this fits into the usual descending approach rather than contradicts it, Example 1y adds an extra note to either side of the lick, keeping the picking of the original portion the same.

Example 1x:

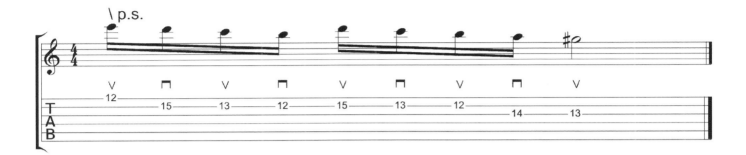

Example 1y:

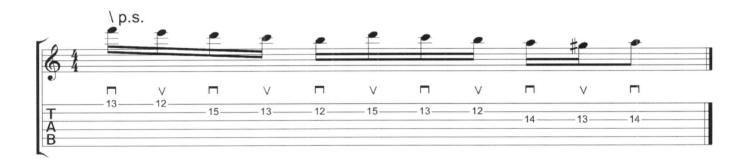

The lone note strategy will play a big part in the loop and sequence drills coming up in Chapter Six.

Biomechanics Summary

It has always been my personal view as a musician that anything is replicable if you know how, and that is precisely the motivation behind the detailed breakdown in this chapter. Where one player may appear to display a natural disposition to a concept, another may need to think harder, practise smarter, and spend more time troubleshooting than the first player. Don't be disheartened if you are the latter. Your efforts will pay dividends if you follow the method and remain self-aware.

Demystification is an essential process in our journeys as musicians, so try not to be overwhelmed with the volume of information but, instead, take logical step by logical step. Information and application build the bridge between where you are and where you'd like to be, so make sure each foundation is stable before you lay the next.

Despite the time it might take to naturally put the Malmsteen picking concepts into practice if they are new to you, the principles themselves contain some highly rewarding payoffs and time-savers. On the surface, it would appear that working on different concepts for ascending and descending directions is to work on two unrelated skills. As you'll hopefully have surmised from the principles in this book, true alternate and economy picking also require the player to master a two-pronged approach, mostly in learning equal opposites regarding pick slant, outside picking and inside picking.

The Yng Way system conserves time and energy in the following ways:

- *Allowing continuous downward picking orientation*

- *Standardising the start of each string with a downstroke*

- *Removing the alternation of outside and inside picking*

- *Systemising any exceptions to the norm with slurs and the lone note strategy*

Once you've transformed your knowledge into habits, an intuition about how the system applies to the examples in this book and the Yngwie Malmsteen catalogue at large should develop, thus enabling you to perform the material with success, confidence, and authenticity.

Chapter Two: Tonalities and Signature Sounds

This chapter is your guide to the all-important sounds of the neoclassical rock vocabulary. While Yngwie is adept in improvisation using a variety of *modes*, his signature sounds are most commonly created using variants of the minor scale and its evil cousin, the *Phrygian dominant* mode of *harmonic minor*, as well as a synthetic scale that I refer to later as the *hybrid minor* scale.

Natural Minor Scale or Aeolian Mode

Construction: I, II, bIII, IV, V, bVI, bVII.

Harmony: I min, II dim, ♭III Maj, IV min, V min, ♭VI Maj, ♭VII Maj

The *natural minor* is a diatonic scale that contains semitone steps between degrees II and bIII, and between degrees V and bVI. Since each natural minor scale shares a *key signature* with a corresponding *major scale*, it is sometimes referred to as a *relative* minor. For example, the A minor scale (containing the notes A, B, C, D, E, F, G) is relative to C major (containing C, D, E, F, G, A, B).

This tonality is one of several derivatives of the major scale, called *modes*, which is why it is known to many improvisers in modern music theory as the *Aeolian mode*, the sixth of seven *modes* of the major scale. The natural minor scale is of importance in western music because we most commonly describe music as being in a major key or its relative minor key, depending on where the resolution is emphasised.

To study other modes and their application, check out *Guitar Scales in Context* by Joseph Alexander and published by *Fundamental Changes*.

On a guitar fretboard, the relative minor root note is found three frets below the major scale root note or nine frets above, adding up to the twelve chromatic notes in each octave. The study examples in this book utilise positional and shifting scale patterns, so familiarise yourself with the shapes that follow. These illustrate the A natural minor scale starting on the sixth string, the fifth string, and across the entire fretboard respectively.

A Natural Minor from 6th string root

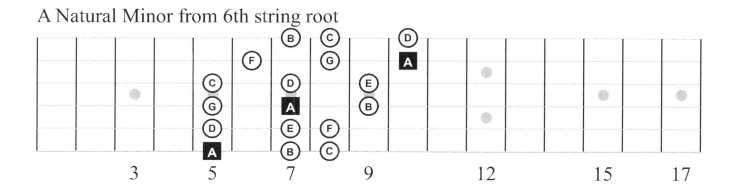

A Natural Minor from 5th string root

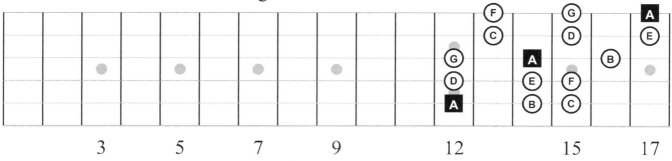

A Natural Minor across the fretboard

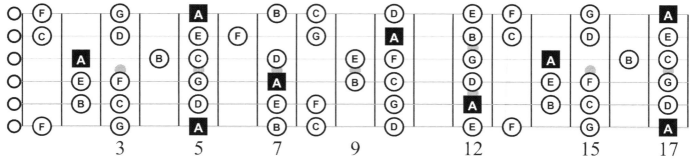

Natural Minor Scale Harmony

By stacking 3rds to build harmony, the natural minor scale produces seven triads which you can use in chord progressions underneath improvisation. Treating each scale degree as the root note of a cluster and adding a diatonic 3rd interval above it, and another diatonic 3rd interval above that results in a chord-scale. In the key of A minor, that produces the following:

A minor (containing the notes A, C, E)

B diminished (containing the notes B, D, F)

C Major (containing the notes C, E, G)

D minor (containing the notes D, F, A)

E minor (containing the notes E, G, B)

F Major (containing the notes F, A, C)

G Major (containing the notes G, B, D)

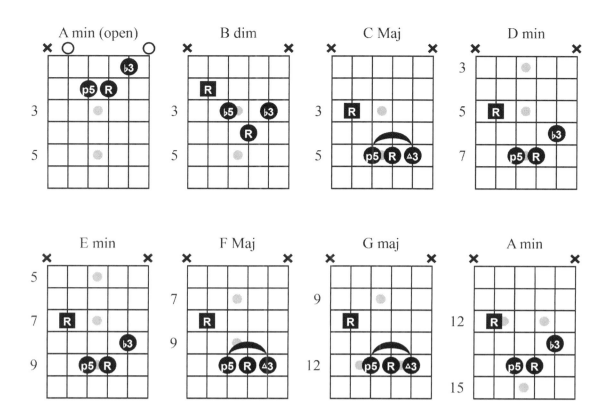

Harmonic Minor Scale

Description: Natural minor with a raised 7th

Construction: I, II, bIII, IV, V, bVI, VII.

Harmony: I min, II dim, bIII Aug, IV min, V Maj, bVI Maj, VII dim.

The harmonic minor scale not only features prominently in the works of The Great Composers that influenced a young Yngwie Malmsteen's approach to composition but also in a lot of Malmsteen's improvisation, where it has become a distinct calling card of his fire-breathing solos. Even more so, harmonic minor's evil twin, the Phrygian dominant mode, is a staple you can just about bet money on appearing in any Malmsteen track.

The harmonic minor scale contains the first six scale degrees of the natural minor but concludes with a major 7th (VII) instead of a minor 7th (bVII). There is a harmonic purpose behind this alteration, which is to create a much stronger resolution from the V Maj chord (which features a major 3rd rather than a minor 3rd) to the I chord. This is called a *perfect cadence*. To hear the impact of this change, play an E minor chord followed by an A minor chord, then compare it to the pleasing resolution created by an E Major chord moving to an A minor chord. The G# note in the E Major chord becomes a leading tone to the A note.

Other engaging sounds in the harmonic minor scale include the exotic effect created by the minor 3rd leap between scale degrees bVI and VII and the fact that the scale also contains the tritones, or diminished 5th intervals, of both degrees.

A Harmonic Minor from 6th string root

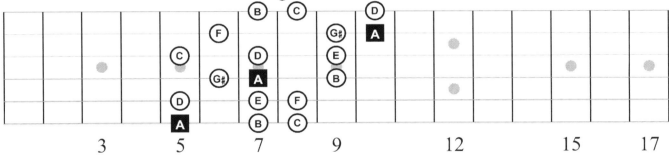

A Harmonic Minor from 5th string root

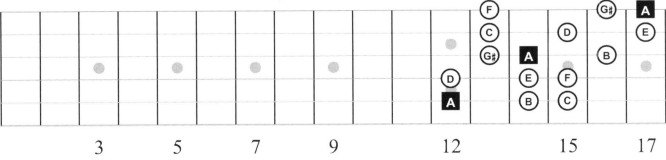

A Harmonic Minor across the fretboard

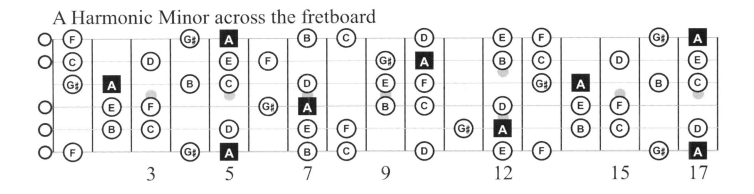

Chord V is not the only element of harmony affected by a change from natural minor to harmonic minor. Chord III Maj will become III Aug, and chord VII Maj will become VII dim (a semitone higher than its original root), giving us the following sequence of triads in the example key of A minor:

A minor (containing the notes A, C, E)

B diminished (containing the notes B, D, F)

C Augmented (containing the notes C, E, G#)

D minor (containing the notes D, F, A)

E Major (containing the notes E, G#, B)

F Major (containing the notes F, A, C)

G# diminished (containing the notes G#, B, D)

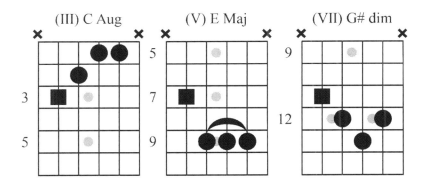

Because the natural minor and harmonic minor scales produce the same I min (and indeed the II dim, IV min and VI Maj triads), it's common for Yngwie to switch between both scales in improvisation over one-chord vamps without hitting any harmonic clams. Don't be alarmed if you see scale runs that include a bVII in one octave and a VII in the next.

Yngwie often composes and improvises around the I min and V Maj chords, the latter of which sets up perhaps the most critical Malmsteen sound, Phrygian dominant.

Phrygian Dominant Mode

Description: The fifth mode of the harmonic minor scale.

Construction: I, bII, III, IV, V, bVI, bVII.

Harmony: I Maj, bII Maj, III dim, IV min, V dim, bVI Aug, bVII minor

With its emphasis on the V chord of harmonic minor (which now becomes the I chord in context), the Phrygian dominant mode affords Yngwie the vehicle to create dark and exotic riffs and solos in an instantly recognisable way that utilises the harmonic minor scale's fifth mode. Rather than merely using the mode as a transitional device to resolve to the minor tonic chord, Yngwie composes sections and solos at length using Phrygian dominant in a modal fashion, exploring its tonality without feeling the need for a perfect cadence resolution each time.

As a mode of A harmonic minor, the E Phrygian dominant mode contains the notes E (I), F (bII), G# (III), A (IV), B (V), C (bVI) and D (bVII). Notice that each of the notes in the modal tonic triad has a semitone interval above it within the scale. Trills between these chord tones and their upward neighbour notes can be an excellent way to spell out the tonality of the mode.

E Phrygian Dominant mode across the fretboard

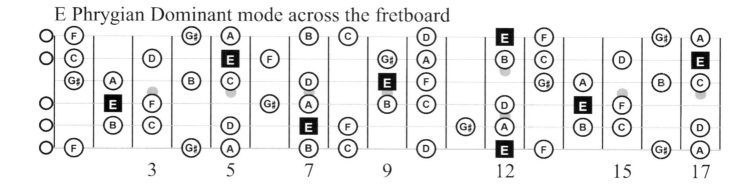

The cornerstone of good modal improvisation is thinking within the tonality at hand, so while the notes of a harmonic minor scale and the derivative Phrygian dominant are the same, it's important to think in context. Consider each note's relationship to the chord beneath, and create ideas that sound good over each chord. To that end, Yngwie favours patterns like Examples 2a and 2b within Phrygian dominant for their emphasis on its tonic triad tones, traversing the fretboard with combinations of three notes and four notes per string.

Example 2a:

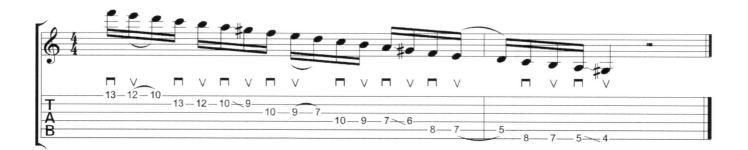

Example 2b:

Diminished 7th Arpeggios

Along with the darker sound of Phrygian dominant, *Diminished 7th arpeggios* are also a Malmsteen neoclassical signature sound. A diminished 7th arpeggio is made up of four notes that are each a minor 3rd away from each other. Phrygian dominant produces four of these which are, in fact, the same notes but inversions of each other. These are located on the bII, III, V and bVII degrees of the mode, manifesting in E Phrygian dominant as:

F Diminished 7 (containing the notes F, G#, B, D)

G# Diminished 7 (containing the notes G#, B, D, F)

B Diminished 7 (containing the notes B, D, F, G#)

D Diminished 7 (containing the notes D, F, G#, B)

The chord spelling of a diminished 7th arpeggio is I, bIII, bV, bbVII and to be enharmonically correct the note spellings above *should* be different. However, since the four arpeggios above are also inversions of each other, another way to look at them in the context of Phrygian dominant is as part of a V7b9 chord without its root. In the example key, E7b9 contains the notes E, G#, B, D and F. The root note of any underlying harmony will produce the E note, and all four diminished 7th arpeggios can be superimposed in solos to enhance the tonality and imply the complete chord.

Diminished 7th chord tones across the fretboard

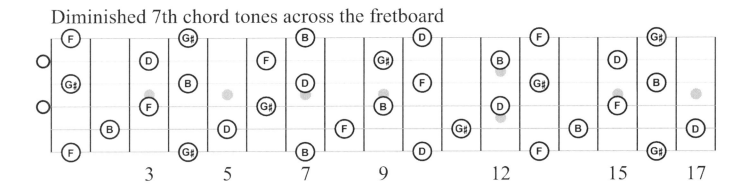

Yngwie often uses sweep picking and position shifting to connect diminished 7th arpeggios up and down the fretboard in minor 3rd steps, like the three-string form below.

Example 2c:

For scale lines like those focused upon in this book, diminished 7th arpeggios can also be used to create the frame of scalar picking patterns. Example 2d outlines a diminished 7th arpeggio with two notes per string, with Example 2e adding a middle note to each string to expand the arpeggio into a Phrygian Dominant line. Try these over an E or E7 chord.

Example 2d:

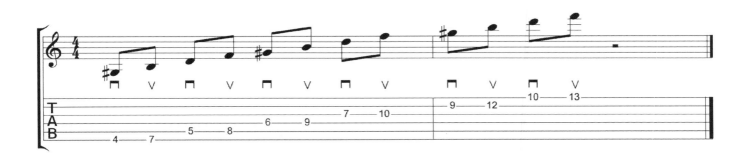

Example 2e:

Hybrid Minor Scale

Description: A synthetic minor scale with eight degrees.

Construction: I, II, bIII, IV, V, bVI, bVII, VII.

Harmony: Use over natural minor or harmonic minor harmony, but be careful!

Hybrid minor is my label for a synthetic scale that occurs in some of Yngwie's best-known scale runs. Whether it evolved as a matter of fretboard convenience, or as a passing tone device, the hybrid minor blurs the lines between natural and harmonic minor scales as both the bVII and VII intervals are present, creating the eight-note scale shown.

A Hybrid Minor from 5th string root

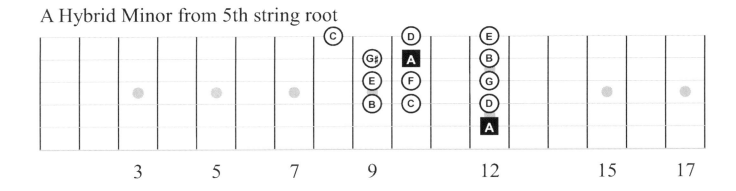

Yngwie uses the hybrid minor effect between the G string and B string, ending the third string on the bVII degree, and beginning the second string on the VII degree. This common occurrence strengthens the case for the pattern evolving as a matter of technical convenience in keeping with three notes on both strings.

In the key of A minor, the hybrid scale will include the notes A, B, C, D, E, F, G and G#. Be careful when using this scale not to hang on to any note that will create dissonance with the chord underneath. For example, when playing an A hybrid minor pattern over an E or E7 chord, use the G note strictly as a passing tone only as it will otherwise cause a direct clash with the G# note in the chord.

Yngwie frequently uses the hybrid minor pattern not only in ascending and descending runs but also in scales sequences like descending fours. It's easy to create a very unusual but recognisable sound when sequencing around the consecutive semitones of the bVII, VII and the root note above them.

Example 2f:

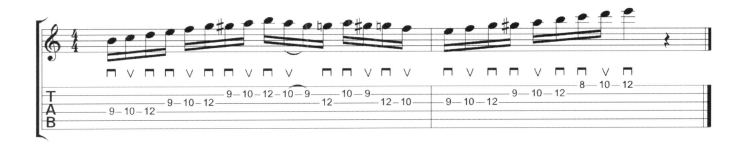

Each of the scales and tonalities mentioned in this chapter can be practised over the relevant tonic chord or by using *drone notes* on the low E or A strings. I recommend free-time improvisation as well as working with the metronome and backing tracks to attune your ears and fingers to the patterns and their relationship to the underlying harmony.

Part Two: Technical Development

Having studied Part One of this book, you should be familiar with the various elements of motion in Yngwie's picking style using terms grounded in science, as well as the musical terminology that will be used to describe the sounds used in the successive chapters. You should now be able to identify the different motion mechanics at play in Yngwie's style and know the sounds and fingerings of the natural, harmonic and hybrid minor scales, the Phrygian dominant mode, and diminished 7th arpeggios.

Part Two puts the mechanical precepts into practice with a series of development drills. I have categorised them into four areas of focus for progressive mastery of the entire system.

- *Single-string and Even Numbers Alternate picking*

- *Ascending Economy Picking*

- *Descending Pick-gato (alternate picking plus legato)*

- *Loops and Sequences*

For the best results, your practice routines should consist of a cross between single and multiple subjects per session. Develop one area in your *focus sessions* and cover numerous areas in *mixed sessions*. A sample development program may look something like this:

Week 1:

- Day 1: Get an overview of the entire system by taking a peek at each chapter in this part

- Days 2-6: Thirty minutes per day working through the first subject at various speeds

- Day 7: Twenty minutes of revision plus ten minutes on the beginning drills of the following chapter

Week 2-4:

- Day 1: Ten-minute review of previous material and twenty minutes working on the new chapter

- Days 2-6: Thirty minutes of focused workouts on the new chapter at various speeds with a metronome

- Day 7: Twenty minutes of revision plus ten minutes on the first few drills of the following chapter

Week 5:

- All days: work up to your clean top speed of the last few drills of each chapter with a metronome

- Take note of any issues and revise the appropriate exercises to overcome them

Week 6 and on:

- Tackle the advanced studies in Part Three, using Part Two as your warm-up material as required

Chapter Three: Single-String and Even Numbers Alternate Picking

Developing robust single-string technique is a crucial part of mastering speed picking. Not only is it a stylistic element of Yngwie's lead playing, but focusing on single string work allows you to excel at several critical technical facets before string changing becomes a factor. Even-numbered multi-string drills will also be introduced in this chapter to demonstrate how you can expand many of the single-string ideas.

The examples in this section are designed to give you the control, synchronisation, speed and timing that will put you in good stead for future chapters. I've created each drill with the aim of building your skillset progressively. When you can execute each one cleanly, accurately and with a degree of confidence, move on to the next.

Regarding Yngwie's fingering preferences, there are two fixed and two alternating fingerings in regular use. When three notes are spaced out starting with a semitone and a wider interval like a whole tone or minor third (Figure 2a), or two consecutive whole tones (Figure 2b), fingers one, two and four are used.

Figure 2a

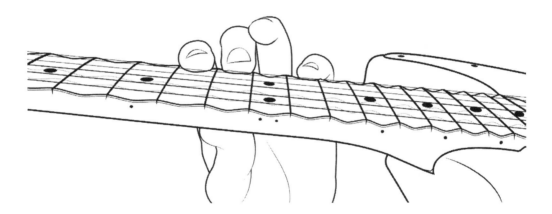

Figure 2b:

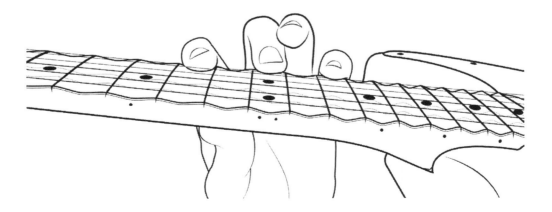

Yngwie handles note-spreads that end with a semitone in two different ways. When using a note spacing like a whole tone to a semitone in isolation, Yngwie favours fingers one, two and three (Figure 2c). For other lines and sequences where it's the logical thing to do so, he instead uses the fourth finger for the higher note and the third finger for the middle note (Figure 2d). Feel free to use either or both at your discretion, so long as you apply your choices with consistency to avoid confusion.

Figure 2c:

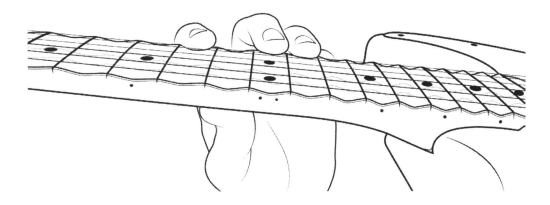

Figure 2d:

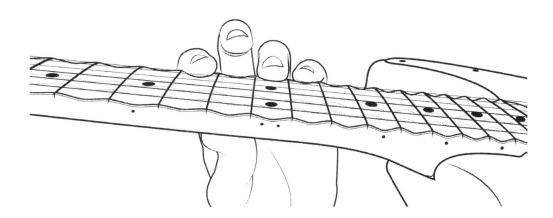

Using the picking hand principles previously covered, work on all drills in the order presented. Work on them *without* a metronome at first because this is about motor skill development. Introduce the metronome to track your progress and ensure you are playing in time once the mechanics are stable. I also suggest tapping your foot on the 1/4 note beats using the foot opposite to your picking hand. Diagonally-opposite limbs often work well together to reinforce internal rhythm, as they do in walking or running.

After a few repeats, move each exercise to the other strings of the guitar one by one, paying adequate attention to any strings that feel harder to play than others. Focus on the weak points until each string feels similar in comfort.

Beginning with Example 3a, use the high E string as a rest stroke guide rail for your picking motion along the B string. As you move the drill to each string, do the same with the higher adjacent string. On the high E string there obviously won't be a higher string to rest on, so be sure that your angles are consistent with what you did on the other strings. Focus only on your picking hand at this stage, as you incorporate pick edge offset, downward picking orientation, and anchored forearm rotation.

Example 3a:

After you've completed the first drill at various speeds and on all strings, add variety in pitch and extra fingers. Remember that you have two choices for fingering with this spacing.

Example 3b:

Examples 3c and 3d are designed to familiarise you with the natural minor scale along one string starting by moving a simple motif up and down diatonically. The 1/4 notes on beats 2 and 4 allow you to shift positions with plenty of time. Stay with the guide rail concept at this point.

Example 3c:

Example 3d:

To ease into playing a steady flow of 1/16th notes along one string with position shifts, the chromatic crawling pattern of Example 3e, (which I call *The Centipede)*, will build your picking hand endurance. The index finger leads each ascending group of four notes, and the fourth finger leads the descent. Aim for at least four clean repeats on each string before attempting a higher tempo, and keep track of the tempo where it falls apart to monitor your progress.

Example 3e:

The Bumblebee-style endurance drill of Example 3f involves all six strings, wider position shifts between chromatic groups, and the fourth finger leading consistently. It is crucial that DPO is used to facilitate each descending string change. Make sure that your exit upstroke on the higher string sets up the entry downstroke of the next string without the need for any second movement.

Example 3f

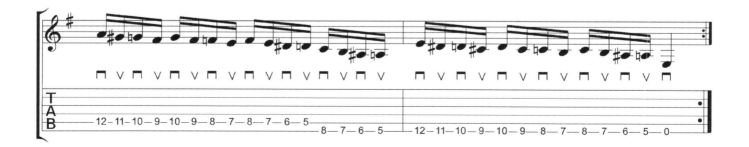

Ascending and descending fours are the staples of an excellent diatonic sequence repertoire, and in the next two examples, three notes from each position are extended with a shift to an additional note in the next position. Ensure that each shift synchronises with the pick stroke to avoid the fourth note of each group sounding twice. A good way to lock in your timing is to accent the downstroke that begins each unit of the sequence.

In the ascending fours of Example 3g, the index finger should synchronise with each beat of the bar. In the descending fours of Example 3h, the finger that hits each beat will depend upon your fingering preference for the *whole tone – semitone* spacing.

Example 3g:

Example 3h:

A sequence I describe as 3-1-2-3 is closely related to ascending fours, but the presence of an extra note at the beginning pushes the ascending fours portion back by one 1/16th note and reverses the picking strokes. Each position shift in Example 3i occurs at the start of each new beat and on a downstroke.

Example 3i:

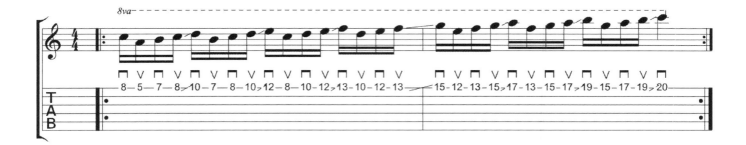

Likewise, the 1-3-2-1 descending counterpart of the previous example is a relation of the descending fours lick, consisting of position shifts at the beginning of each new beat.

Example 3j:

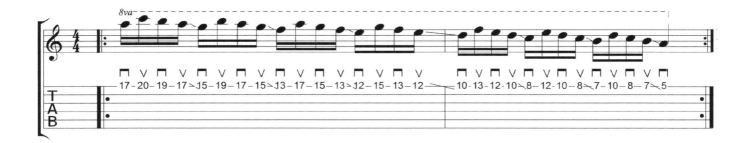

Keep in mind that sequences like 3-1-2-3 and 1-3-2-1 can be used with wider jumps along strings also, as Example 3k in A harmonic minor demonstrates.

Example 3k:

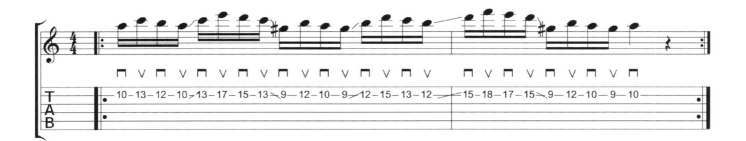

One of Yngwie's most familiar single-string licks is something I call the *Sixes Ostinato*. It appears on single and multiple strings in Yngwie's solos. In this iteration, the highest note alternates between the 13th fret C note and the 15th fret D note. Pay close attention to the suggested fingering to avoid getting knotted up. The ostinato works as a 1/16th note (Example 3l) or sextuplet (Example 3m) phrase.

Example 3l

Example 3m

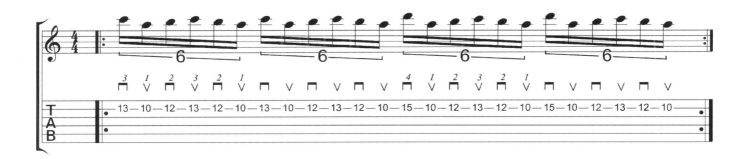

Example 1n is a multi-string expansion of the sixes ostinato which uses the two-string diminished 7th arpeggio form to outline an E Phrygian dominant tonality.

Example 3n:

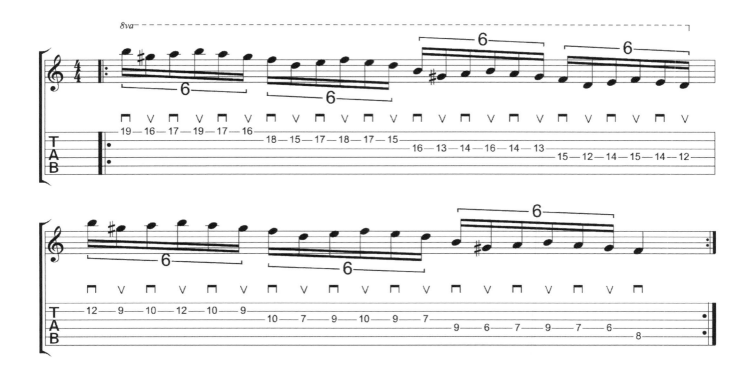

The final drill of your practice routine for this chapter is a pedal-point etude in the style of J.S. Bach, and a chance to apply your picking chops, fretboard knowledge and position shifting into one exercise. Transpose it to different keys, octaves and strings to challenge yourself. The notated key is A minor with some modulation.

Example 3o

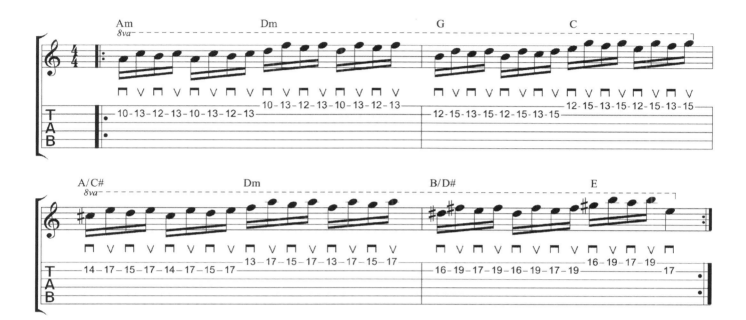

Chapter Four: Ascending Economy Picking Drills

The ascending economy picking drills in this chapter will help you develop and refine the first of two elements in Yngwie's asymmetrical string-changing system for odd numbers. Using sweep picking to finish a lower string and begin a higher string with the same pick stroke is the go-to approach anytime odd numbers of notes per string are involved.

Let's start by looking at how a string change works from the sixth string to the fifth. In Example 4a, a single downstroke sounds both the C and D notes. The sweep should be executed with rest strokes, firstly from the E string to the A string and then from the A string to the D string.

Example 4a:

This string-changing mechanic is the same used in two-string triads. In Example 4b, use an outside pick stroke with DPO to exit the A string and return to the low E string.

Example 4b:

Applying the string change to a scalar situation starts in Example 4c by adding notes on either side. Make sure that the economy-picked downstrokes are neither faster nor slower than the alternate-picked notes.

Example 4c:

In Example 4d, the two alternating phrases each end on upstrokes. Downward picking orientation reinforces the outside picking pathway back to the low E string each time, which will be a valuable tool in the loops and sequences in Chapter Six.

Example 4d:

Example 4e sees a two-string drill develop into a three-octave, six-string pattern by creating diatonic pairs out of strings six and five, five and four, four and three and so on. Each unit of the lick takes up two beats and starts with the fretting hand index finger. Use this example to make sure that you are equally adept at string changing on each string pair.

Example 4e:

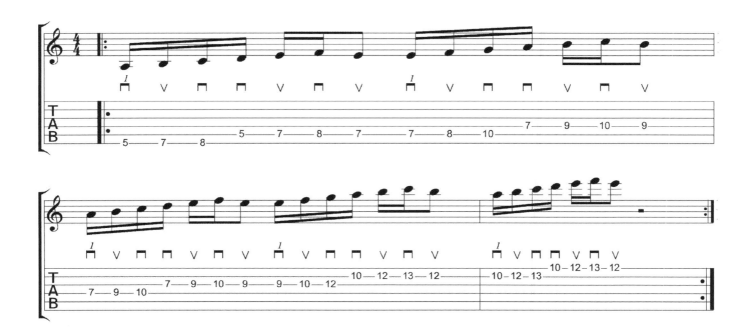

Now that you can move smaller units around the fretboard, it's time to apply the ascending strategy to scale playing. Any odd-numbered form like three-note-per-string scales (referred to herein as *three NPS*) will work perfectly with this approach. In the A natural minor run of Example 4f, pay close attention to the timing as you accelerate the tempo to your top speed. Yngwie will often rush phrases for effect, but its beneficial to your development to stay with the beat at first, applying stylistic acceleration later by choice rather than by accident.

Example 4f:

Since the integration of ideas is such a significant aspect of fluid playing in Yngwie's style, take your time mastering the final development drill in this chapter. Example 4g ascends with the same picking pattern as the first bar of Example 4f but uses an altered fingering described earlier as the *hybrid minor* scale. With this ascent taking you up the 4th beat of bar one, the drill then switches to descending fours down the high E string using the A harmonic minor scale.

You can break this drill into the two elements contained within it for memorising but, since fluidity is the goal, it's best to practise both bars from beginning to end as soon as you're able.

Example 4g:

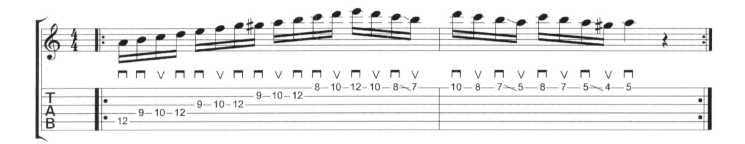

Chapter Five: Descending Pick-gato Drills

The descending drills in this chapter form a practice routine that will help the combination of alternate picking and strategised pull-offs feel like an extension of the even numbers strategy, rather than a contradiction to it.

Before commencing the Pick-gato drills, start with Example 5a, which is designed to wake up your fretting hand using hammer-ons and pull-offs. Repeat this exercise on all the other strings when practising, picking the first note of each bar only. Try to avoid any fluctuation in tempo when your fretting hand no longer has the picking hand to lock into for timing.

Example 5a:

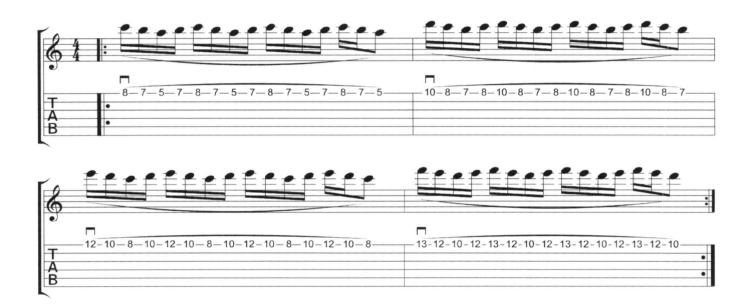

After warming up your fretting hand slurs, bring picking back into play with Example 5b. Incorporating a pull-off into the first triplet of each bar is all it takes to maintain an even number of pick strokes on both strings. After the upstroke preceding each pull-off, your pick should find its way to the next string with ease. If not, double-check your downward pick slant. When you have memorised the pattern, try it on other string pairs like the third and fourth strings, and the fifth and sixth strings.

Example 5b:

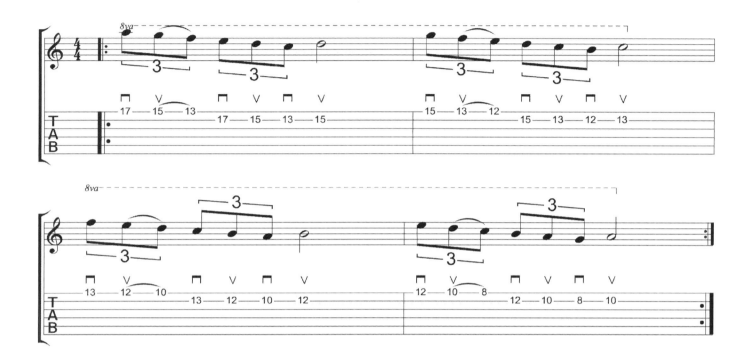

Example 5c once again uses a single pull-off to keep the system together, this time in a two-octave E Phrygian dominant lick. Yngwie stylistically starts smooth and finishes more aggressively with licks such as this, increasing pick attack towards the end of each phrase.

Example 5c:

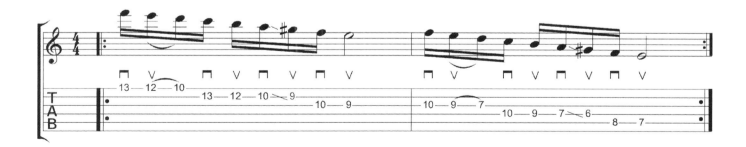

A straightforward scale like the A harmonic minor pattern in Example 5d enables the repetition of the *down, up, pull*-off picking form across multiple strings. Take care to maintain good timing, and try this picking form with all the three NPS scales that you know.

Example 5d:

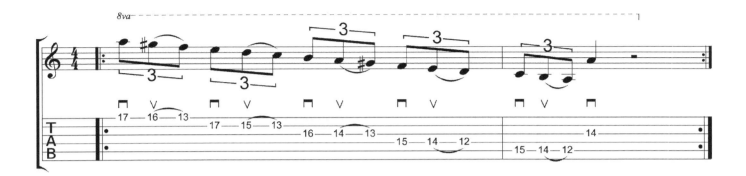

In improvisation, it's important to be able to switch between odd and even numbers with ease, something that the next two examples are designed to target. Using the previous A harmonic minor shape, Examples 5e and 5f mix odds and evens by doubling the triplets on selected strings. In Example 5e, the *down, up, pull-off* form on the first, third and fifth strings is interspersed with the pure alternate picking on the second and fourth strings. Example 5f does the opposite.

Example 5e:

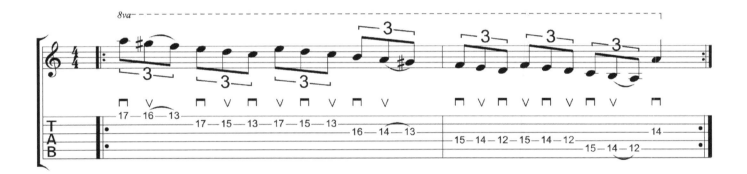

Example 5f:

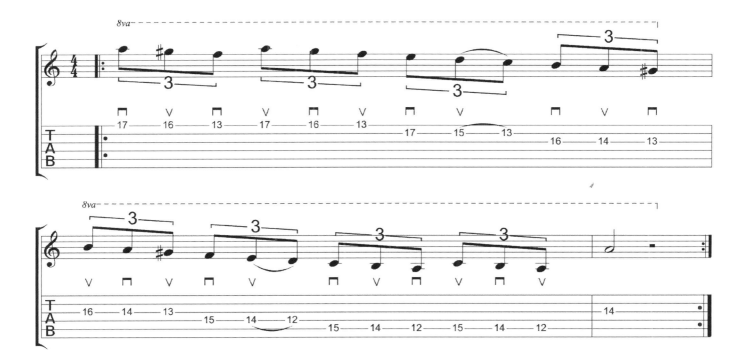

The last goal to accomplish in this chapter is to be able to play through phrases in which the placement of legato notes and string changes are irregular, i.e., not occurring in the same parts of the beat each time. Observe and work with Example 5g very slowly at first, noting where each beat falls as you play through its varying numbers of notes per string. With several slow repeats, you should be able to get a sense of where the pick strokes and pull-offs occur without reading through every time. As you increase the tempo, be vigilant in maintaining the 1/16th note rhythm, taking care to make sure that any three-note portions don't turn into triplets.

Example 5g:

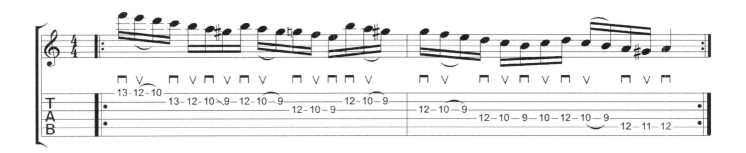

Chapter Six: Loop and Sequence Drills

The purpose of this chapter is to consolidate the information and techniques you have acquired in previous chapters into a series of cyclical and sequenced exercises for practice. Building on the foundations you have created through practising chapters three, four and five, these examples will focus on bolstering your ability to seamlessly combine techniques in a musical way consistent with the Malmsteen style.

Looping is the term I give to playing short phrases that ascend and descend to create tension and interest before venturing into another idea. Yngwie does this frequently especially on the high E and B strings, but you should experiment with the loops here in multiple octaves and scale patterns.

Example 6a combines the ascending and even number strategies with odd numbers on the B string and even numbers on the high E string. Each ascending string change occurs with a sweep and each descending string change occurs after an upstroke with an outside picking path back to the B string. Melodically, this loop starts with four ascending notes and continues with two beats of descending fours, repeating in total after three beats.

Example 6a:

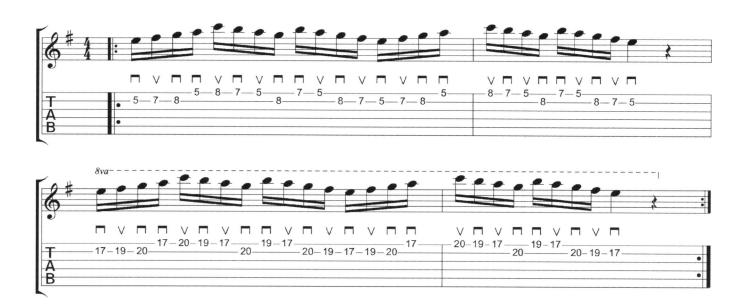

Example 6b, also in E minor, features three beats of descending fours or a 4-3-2-1 sequence, followed by one beat of four ascending 1/16th notes. The technical execution of this loop is a vital facet of the lick because it introduces the idea of a slur and a *crosspicking* stroke to pave the way for the lone note application in the 3rd beat of the bar. The lone note strategy and its setup play a big part in the sequences that follow.

Study this drill by working on beats 3 and 4 at first. This is the more natural half of the lick and a typical way of using the lone note on the high E string. Next, add at the last two 1/16th notes of beat 2 comprised of downstroke on the 10th fret of the B string with a pull-off to the 8th fret.

A subtle crosspicking motion will be required to get on the right side of the high E string for beat 3 by stealthily lifting the hand at the wrist joint (wrist extension). Crosspicking is a movement created by flexion and extension of the wrist to go over a string. It's common in styles like Bluegrass and Country where string changes can be required after single notes per string, but a rarely-detected occurrence in Yngwie's style.

The hammer-on just before the string change allows enough time to get into position without the need to overtly hop over the first string. Enough movement to clear the string is all it takes to preserve the other components of the drill and keep it flowing.

Example 6b:

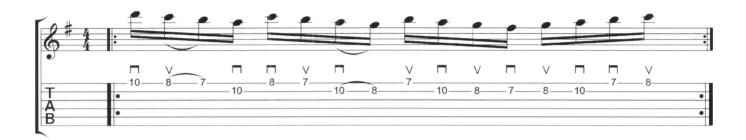

Since you've done all that hard work, let's apply the same form to another loop, this time in E harmonic minor.

Example 6c:

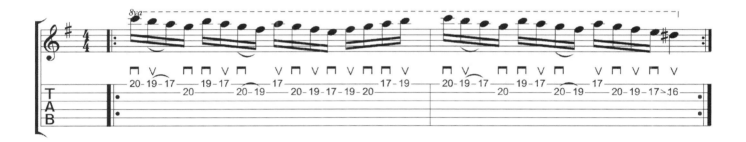

Loops can be a great start to a descending scale, as shown in Example 6f, which takes the drill from Example 6b and adds a descending E minor pattern in bar two where the loop would have otherwise repeated.

Example 6d:

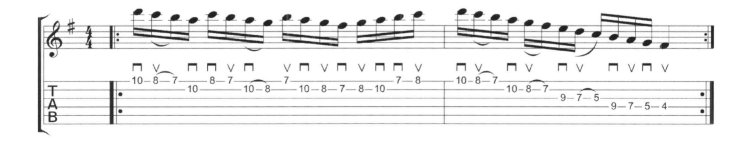

When a descending fours sequence is played all the way through a positional scale pattern like that of Example 6e, it's useful to first take note of three things:

1. There is a repeated layout of notes on each string pair: three notes and one note, two notes and two notes, one note and three notes. After these three steps take place, the layout repeats on the next string pair (starting on the 4th beat of the first bar in this case).

2. The first cycle of three descending fours starts on a downstroke (beats 1-3 of bar one).

3. The ensuing cycles of three descending fours start on upstrokes.

Example 6e:

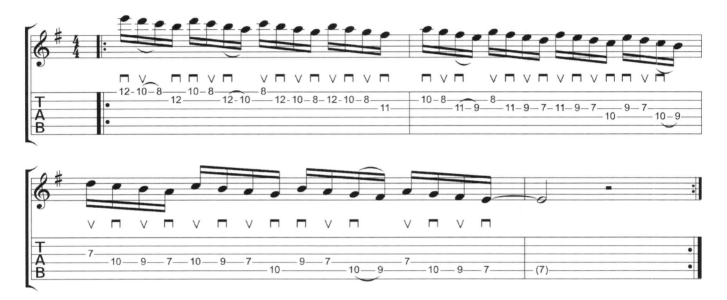

For the sake of uniformity, the previous example could also start with *up, down, up* to bring in line with the subsequent repeats of the sequence (see beat 4 of bar one). However, doing so won't always be an option depending on the licks leading into such a sequence, as Example 6g will reinforce.

Yngwie favours fretboard patterns that don't require finger rolling or awkward position shifts in sequencing. Don't we all? To thwart fingering inconveniences, Yngwie uses single-string descending fours to locate and descend in his preferred patterns. Example 6f uses one such inconvenient pattern, remedied in Example 6g with a more finger-friendly pattern using the same notes.

Example 6f:

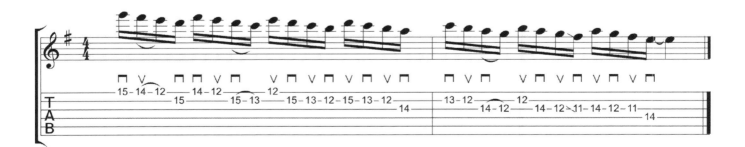

Instead, let's use single-string position shifts to locate a familiar shape in Example 6g. The single-string descending fours in beats 1 and 2 of the first bar again dictate that the positional element of the sequence on beat 3 begins on a downstroke.

Example 6g:

Ascending Sequences

Some of the most commonly used ascending sequences in Yngwie's playing are the 1-2-3-1 and 3-1-2-3 forms, both of which are permutations of the ascending fours or 1-2-3-4 sequence, as the next few drills highlight.

Example 6h uses the 1-2-3-1 sequence, meaning that each unit of four notes contains three ascending notes, followed by a return to the first note. The sequence then moves up to the second degree of the scale from which the 1-2-3-1 unit is reiterated and so on.

The lone note exception occurs in ascending sequences just like it does in descending examples, handled with an upstroke and preceded this time by a hammer-on. In this drill, the lone note first occurs on the third 1/16th note of beat 2, bar one.

Example 6h:

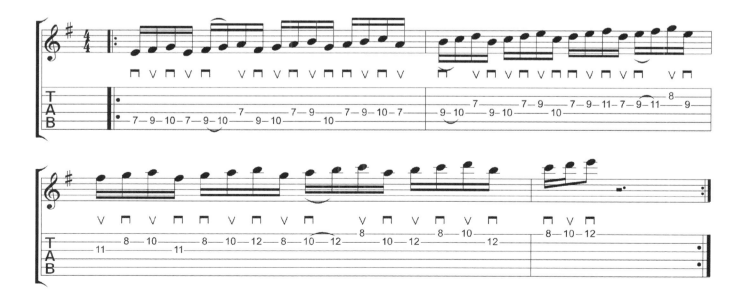

One of the best payoffs to learning the sequencing aspect of Yngwie's system is the continuity of picking that emerges when learning derivatives of an idea already studied. Examples 6i and 6j are cases in point. At first glance, the 3-1-2-3 layout of Example 6i might seem like a new sequence. It is, in fact, the result of dropping the first two 1/16th notes of Example 6h and starting what remains from the 1st beat of the bar. By removing those notes while leaving the pick strokes as they were, we can form a new musical idea from an existing mechanical template.

Example 6i:

Next, by removing the first *three* 1/16th notes of Example 6h and keeping the applicable pick strokes intact, an ascending fours sequence is revealed.

Example 6j:

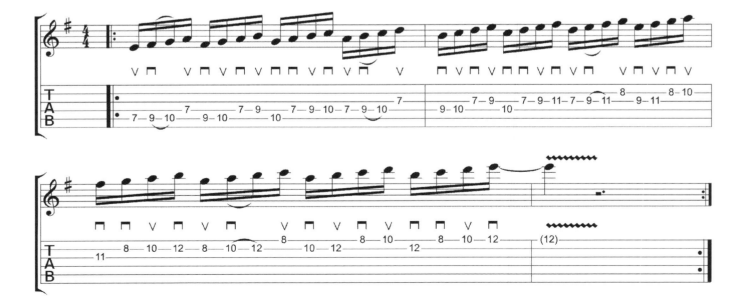

While the beginning upstroke of the last example is consistent with its permutation of the previous examples, being able to start it on a downstroke on the fly in improvisation is also a worthwhile option to keep up your sleeve. In your practice, try alternating the first bar of Example 6j with this substitute measure.

Example 6k:

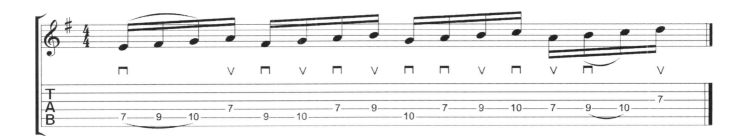

Combining single-string and positional ascending sequences is an excellent way to build an idea beyond the limits of either. Your goal for sequences like Example 6l is to create a seamless ascent as the single-string position-shifts on the third and first strings are brought together by the positional increments in bar two and the first half of bar three. This drill is again in the key of E minor but suits the tonality of C Lydian, built upon the VI degree of E minor or IV degree of G Major.

Example 6l:

Chapter Seven: Picking Decryption

These examples will test your perception of how lines should be executed using The Yng Way. At first, the examples are presented without pick strokes or slurring indicators. Peruse each phrase before reaching for your guitar to see if you can decode the picking solution that matches the principles in this book. Next, test your hypothesis and conclude, or reassess until satisfied.

Example 7a:

Example 7b:

Example 7c:

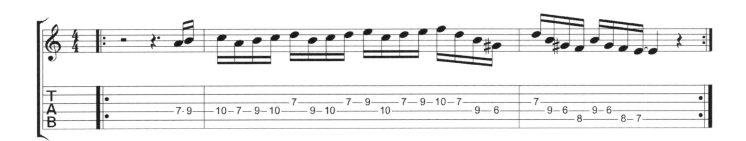

On the next page, the same examples have been decoded with Yngwie-compliant pick strokes and slurs, as well as the decryption keys used.

Solutions for Chapter Seven Examples

Below are the completed versions of Examples 7a, 7b and 7c. Each lick now has picking and slurs indicated, plus the decryption key that corresponds to the decision made with each string change.

Decryption keys:

EC = Economy-picked string change (ascending strategy)

PU = Pull-off after an even number of alternate picking strokes (descending strategy)

LN = Upstroke preceded by a hammer-on or pull-off (lone note exception)

Example 7a Picking Solution:

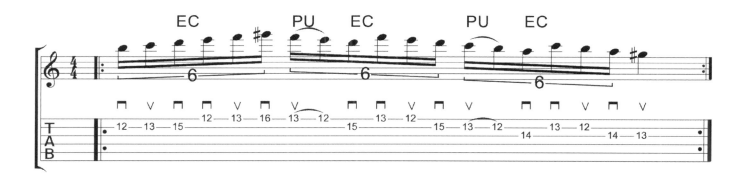

Example 7b Picking Solution:

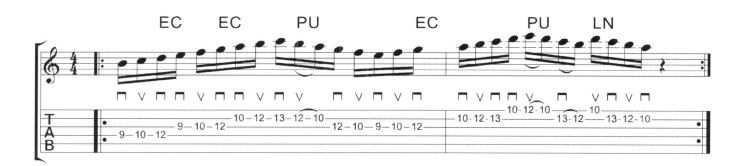

Example 7c Picking Solution:

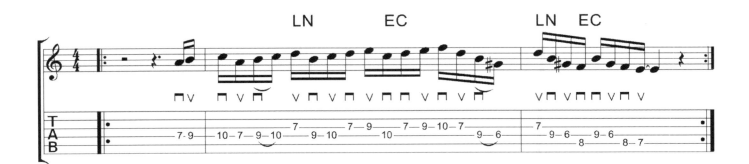

If your intuition served you correctly, you have done well! If not, study the differences between your conclusion and the answers presented. More deductive reasoning awaits you in the transcriptions of Yngwie's music online and in books, so be sure to spend some time on the written medium of his music, outside of studying this book.

Part Three is a collection of authentic-sounding lines in the Malmsteen style that will build upon the skillset you have created throughout Part Two.

Part Three: Advanced Studies

It's time to put all the methods, sounds and expertise you've acquired into more extended passages that would be right at home in an Yngwie-esque solo. While perfect for practice material just as a violinist hones his or her chops on Kreutzer or Paganini themes, it is primarily intended for you to use these phrases in actual music and improvisation.

Each study is discussed in terms relating to:

- *Musical attributes*

- *Pressure points that may require extra attention in practice*

- *Mechanical Sub-concepts that augment ideas covered in previous chapters*

I have grouped these studies according to musical key, but it's essential to your progress a musician that you transpose your favourite ideas to many keys.

Chapter Eight: Studies in E Minor

Study 1 (Example 8a)

The core element in this study is a three-and-a-bit-octave harmonic minor pattern, one of Yngwie's signature *One-Way* layouts. It is only ever used this way in descending. Each octave takes place on two strings, one string containing four notes and the other containing three, except for a position shift on the low E string to access three additional notes.

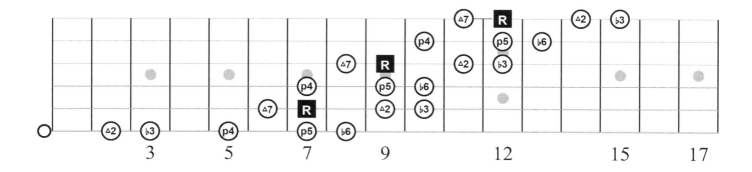

Playing this pattern high to low with alternate picking would result in each octave having opposite pick strokes to the next. The Yng Way enables a consistent approach to the pattern that is not thrown off-course by the interchange of even and odd numbers of notes per string.

In Example 8a, the scale is preceded by a melodic motif that also repeats in octaves, beginning on the third 1/8th note of bar one, beat 3 and ending on the first note of the descending scale in bar three. The index finger should initiate each four-note iteration of the ascending motif. In bars three and four, lead each descending stage with either the third or fourth finger as per your fingering preference. Yngwie uses this pattern over the tonic triad of a minor key.

Example 8a:

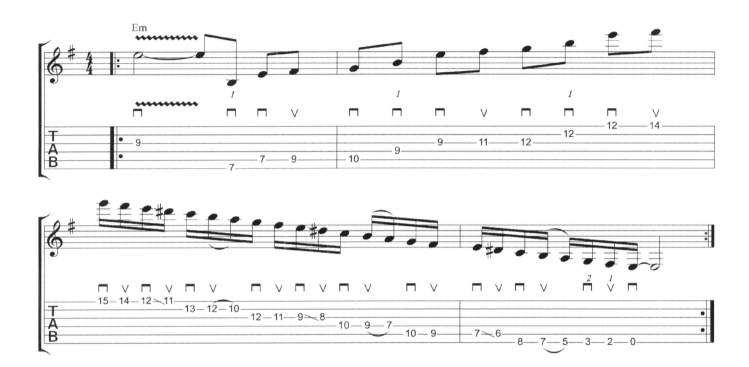

Study 2 (Example 8b)

Being able to re-contextualise your ideas is an important skill to have, and the next two studies provide examples of doing. Using the descending scale portion of the previous study as a fingering framework, Example 8b shifts its tonal emphasis to the B Phrygian dominant mode of E harmonic minor, resolving to a B note on the last 1/16th note of bar two. A short *tail* in bars three and four fills out the remaining bars and emphasises the Phrygian dominant characteristics of bII and III intervals.

The position-shifting ostinato in bar one can be used a drill on its own until you can pick it at the same speed as the rest of the pattern. The index finger takes care of the downward position shifts from frets 12 to 11 and, for most players, the fourth finger will feel the most comfortable handling the upward position changes from frets 14 to 15. Focus on your timing, particularly in taking care not to waver from evenly-picked 1/16th notes on the high E string.

Example 8b:

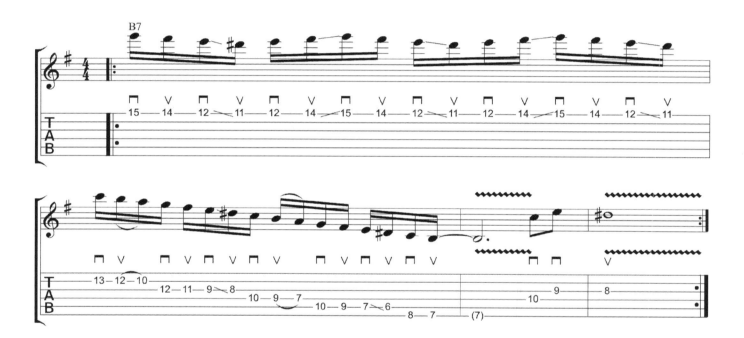

Study 3 (Example 8c)

Just as a long stretch of highway has multiple on-ramps and off-ramps, Yngwie's favourite scale shapes form a route that can be entered and exited at various points. Such usage allows both familiarity and variety, maximising the functionality of a pattern without being limited to it.

In this B Phrygian dominant study, a 1-3-2-1 sequence on the high E string steps down from the 17th fret, arriving at the original E minor *highway* in bar two where another two steps of 1-3-2-1 occur. The line travels straight down the B and G strings as usual before hanging on to the D# note that ends bar two.

After the sustaining the D# note into the beginning of bar three, a detour from the highway occurs in the form of another 1-3-2-1 sequence on the G string. The fourth bar sees a return to the familiar descending pattern, concluding on the B note on the 7th fret on the low E string.

Developing detours like these is an excellent way to know your fretboard better while also taking advantage of patterns that work well for you. This run is well-suited to a B7 chord or a B Phrygian Dominant riff like *Now Your Ships Are Burned*.

Example 8c:

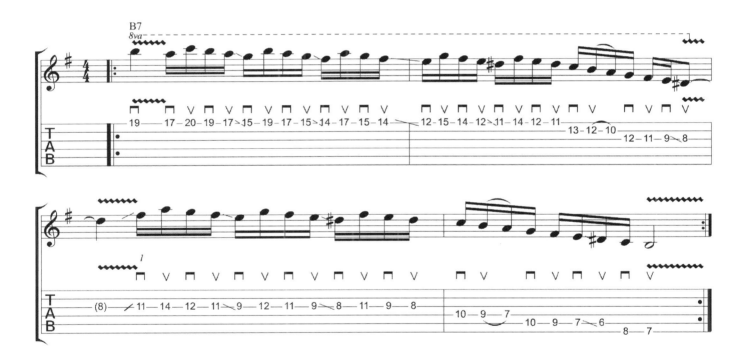

Study 4 (Example 8d)

Let's expand on the fretboard coverage with two new patterns. This study combines descending runs that are not only phrased identically in the example but are diatonic 3rds apart, meaning either can function as a harmony line for the other.

Punctuated by *imperfect cadences* (chord I to chord V) in E minor, both runs are based on 1/8th note triplets except for one beat of four 1/16th notes that begin each descent. The triplet rhythm also lends itself to a fast shuffle or 12/8 time signature. Using the faster-starting notes is a standard Yngwie expression tool used to create interest and get things started with a bang. Also characteristic in its delivery is the trait of using a single upstroke followed by legato on the four starter notes, a variation of the lone note exception.

While the fingering of the first descending pattern is yet another integration of four and three notes per string, its counterpart in the fourth bar has four notes on the B string and only two notes on the G string. The difference in layout is because Yngwie always sources the VII degree of the harmonic minor from the B string this in shape string rather than with the comparatively cumbersome reach for the same note on the G string. Besides being a more user-friendly fingering this way, The Yng Way is set up in such a way that you can play any number of notes per string without breaking the technical systems in place.

Example 8d:

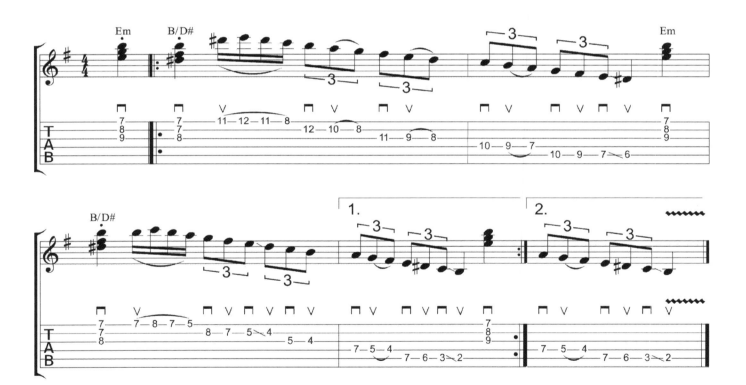

Study 5 (Example 8e)

The hybrid minor shape is one of the few patterns that Yngwie uses in both ascending and descending circumstances. The consecutive semitone intervals between the bVII, VII and I degrees create an attention-grabbing chromatic passing tone sound, particularly in sequencing as you travel back and forth through these three scale degrees.

In this study, bar one consists of a looping lick on the first two strings, comprised of three units of descending fours followed by four consecutive ascending notes bringing it back to the 19th fret of the high E string in bar two. Bars two, three and four consist entirely of descending fours from the high E string to the A string. For extra anticipation, bar one can be repeated as many times as you like before releasing the tension in the last bars.

You can use this pattern and sequence over the V or I chord in E minor. If choosing the latter, omit the last D# note at the end of bar four to create resolution over the E minor chord, or swap the order of the D# and the E notes on the fifth string.

Example 8e:

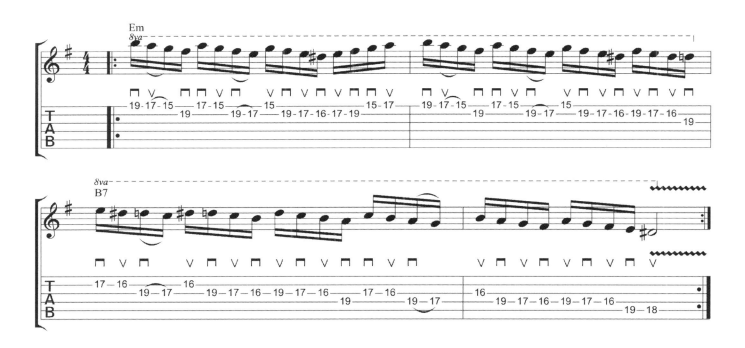

Chapter Nine: Studies in A Minor

Study 6 (Example 9a)

By transposing a couple of previously-featured patterns to the key A minor, this study begins with an ascent of the hybrid minor framework used in Example 8e. It ends with a descent of the harmonic minor pattern from Example 8a and uses a single-string natural minor sequence to connect the two. It is common for Yngwie's lines to combine the attributes of multiple minor scales in extended phrases like this example.

The ascending run in bar one uses the archetypal ascending picking strategy through beats 1, 2 and 3. On beat 4 of the first bar, a 3-1-2-3 sequence traverses positions eight to seventeen along the high E string using notes from the A natural minor scale. In bar three, Yngwie's much-used sixes ostinato takes places between the 17th and 20th frets and again between the 16th and 19th frets. Complying with the sequence numbering system in this book, I think of the sixes ostinato as 3-1-2-3-2-1.

The descending harmonic minor pattern used from the 4th beat of bar three to the end of bar four should feel very familiar by now, having used its E minor version in Studies 1, 2 and 3.

Example 9a:

Study 7 (Example 9b)

This E Phrygian dominant study is a rapid-fire exercise in alternate picking, enabled by even numbers of notes per string that allow you to pick every note with ferocity. Yngwie has been known to shred this kind of run on both acoustic and electric to good effect. When played over backings that have a half-time feel, the run will create the effect of 1/32nd notes, which Yngwie uses for drama and contrast over slower backings.

The tremolo-picked high E note in the first half of bar one allows you to set the picking hand in motion before hitting the three-octave descending pattern that covers all strings and concludes on the open low E string. Like the three-octave harmonic minor map used in previous examples, this shape contains seven notes between each string pair. This time, however, it's three notes on the higher string and four notes on the lower. For consistency, start the E note in each octave with the same finger. For Yngwie, that means the second finger.

Example 9b:

Study 8 (Example 9c)

Something to remember when picking within the system of this book is that string layout determines what pick strokes are used rather than the rhythmic location of notes within the bars or beats. Some examples might create a temporary sense of displacement as a result, but the benefits of mechanical consistency will soon replace it. This study is a case in point.

As a result of the nine pick-up notes in bar one, upstrokes are brought about on the first 1/8th note triplet of each subsequent bar, which might seem like an odd proposition at first. Taking into account the last of those pick-up notes (the 12th fret high E note at the end of bar one), what we have is the same picking sequence as Example 9b, reconfigured from 1/16th notes to 1/8th note triplets.

The task, therefore, is to get your brain aligned with the way the existing mechanics apply to different beat divisions and starting points. The only change for your fretting hand is the position shift from the last pick-up note to the first note of bar two.

Example 9c:

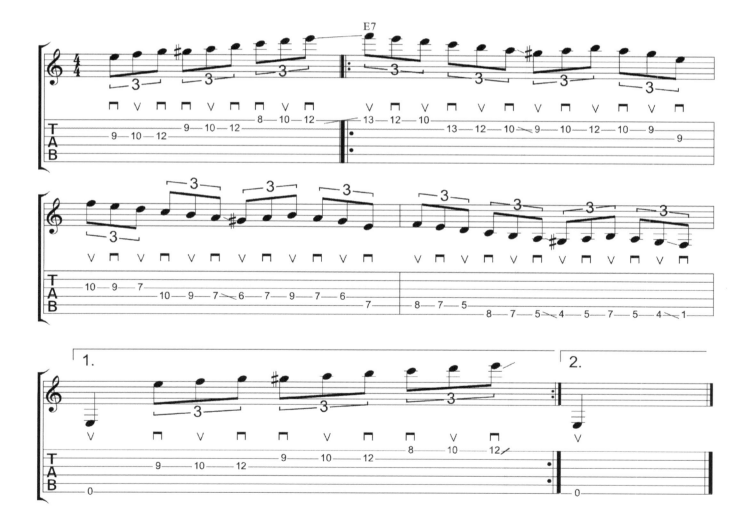

Study 9 (Example 9d)

After the descending even numbers in the last two examples, this alternate-picked study uses the sixes ostinato across all six strings. It begins with three occurrences of the ostinato on the high E string in bar one but replaces the initial F note with a G# on the first sextuplet of beats 2 and 3. For ease of fingering on this first-string portion, assign your third finger to the 13th fret of the E string and fourth finger to the 16th fret rather than using the fourth finger to jump back and forth three frets at a time.

Example 9d:

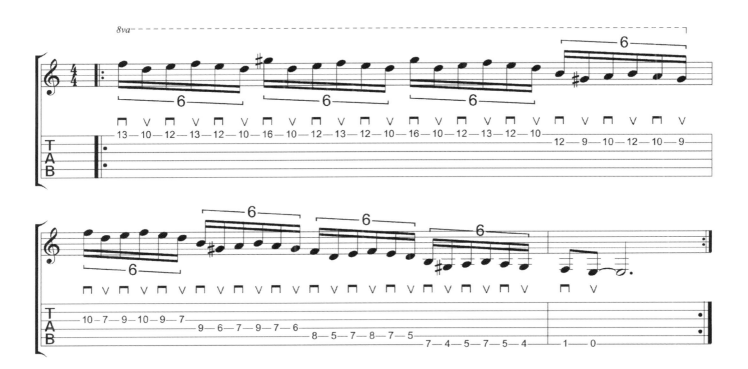

Study 10 (Example 9e)

This ascending study, which fits nicely into any three NPS layout, makes good use of what I call the *swoop and loop*. Consisting of six-note units in string pairs and phrased in 1/16th notes, the sequence in bars one and two contain three notes on the lower string of each pair, two notes on the higher string and one more note on the lower string before a new unit begins a string higher. The swoop and loop term refers to the string-changing pattern which entails an ascending sweep, an outside pick stroke, and another ascending sweep.

After the first two 1/16th notes of bar one, the picking sequence is a repetition of *down, down, up* until the end of bar two. Bar three features two units of ascending fours in beats 1 and 2, followed by two groups of descending fours in beats 3 and 4. Bar four contains a simple ascending phrase to pad out the line.

Given the six-note span of each repeating unit in this sequence, you should also experiment with playing these notes as 1/8th note triplets and 1/16th note triplets or sextuplets.

Example 9e:

Study 11 (Example 9f)

While not sequentially an *exact* reversal of the previous study, this example begins with a sequence in bars one and two that can serve as a great descending companion to the ascending line that starts Example 9e.

Articulated here in an A harmonic minor / E Phrygian dominant shape spanning frets 10 to 17, this sequence again extends over all six strings using a six-note melodic figure in string pairs. Each six notes are played *down, up, pull-off, down, down, up*. The position shift on the 3rd beat of bar two bypasses the sequence for just one 1/4 note value but beat 4 of the bar sees another occurrence of the six-note figure carrying over into the first two notes in bar three.

For the sake of variation, bars three and four complete the study with a series of 1/8th note triplets and straightforward melodic content from the low E string back up to the G string. You can reconfigure the 1/16th notes of bars one and two to triplet groupings for variation, so experiment!

Example 9f:

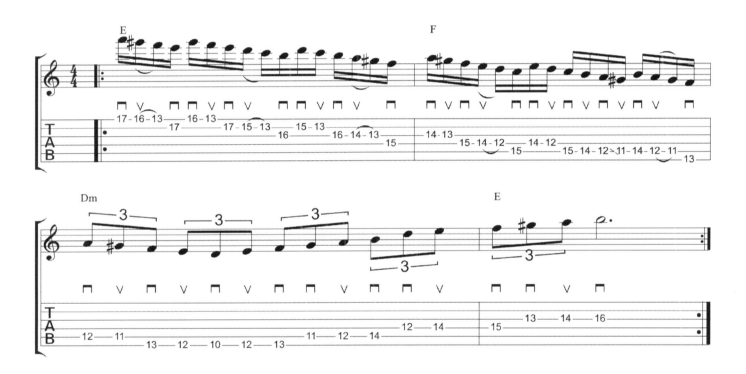

Study 12 (Example 9g)

The ascending portion of this A minor study is all about the application of a sideways position-shifting device I call the *Fives Turnaround*. Yngwie connects various three NPS patterns with this device by dropping a note from an otherwise six-note pattern each time he switches positions. It sets up the picking motion so that the position-shift can take place after an upstroke and begin the next position on a downstroke.

Bar one of this example starts in the A natural minor scale, fifth position. After the upstroke that occurs on the first 1/16th note of beat 2, shift your fretting hand back to the 7th fret of the low E string with the index finger. Doing so is the standard move in the fives turnaround.

You can continue to ascend three notes per string and apply the turnaround strategy each time you wish to switch positions on the same string pair. In this study, two more position shifts are set up with groups of five on the D and G strings, and B and E strings as indicated. A descending fours sequence completes the study in bars three and four.

Example 9g:

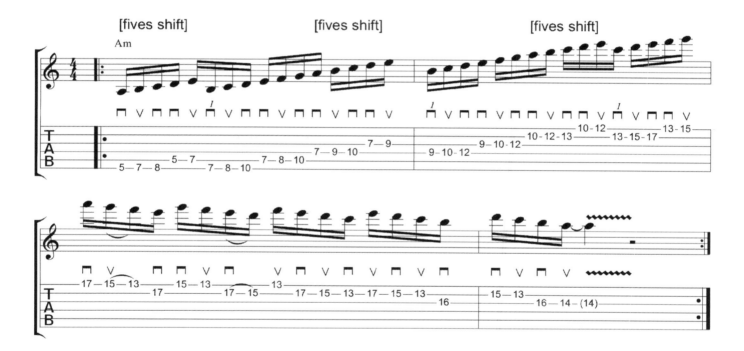

Study 13 (Example 9h)

A downward position-shifting habit of Yngwie's is what I call *Lateral Tens*. He will play ten notes up and down a pair of strings (usually the high E and B strings), but instead of returning to the starting note, a new set of ten begins one diatonic position lower. The Lateral Tens can occur in a standalone lick, or in the case of this study, appear after an ascending lead-up.

Ignoring the note groupings for a moment, take a look at the B string and high E string portions of the first bar in Example 9h. Here is an isolated lateral ten unit that can be practised as a loop to get accustomed to the combination of the ascending sweep, hammer-ons and pull-offs, and two alternate-picked notes back on the B string that is sequenced in units.

After spending some time looping the first lateral ten, proceed to the remaining tens. The second group begins on beat 1 of bar two. The third group begins mid-way through bar two on the 12th fret of the second string, and the last set starts at the beginning of bar three.

Next, it is time to consider the use of tuplets in phrasing. Many of Yngwie's lines contain what may feel like *extra notes* when your experience has thus far been the use of conventional divisions of beats like 1/8th notes, 1/16th notes and triplets thereof. In phrasing examples like *this* study, the focus is not necessarily upon how many notes to squeeze into a beat, but on starting ideas at particular target points within the bars.

The aim here, therefore, is to have a series of motifs that begin on beats 1 and 3 of each bar and apply the necessary acceleration to arrive at the next idea on the target beat. So, the nine ascending 1/16th notes at the beginning of the first bar fit in the space of beats 1 and 2, the first lateral ten (with a couple of extra-rushed legato notes) will be played in beats 3 and 4, and so on.

From beat 3 of the third bar, the phrasing eases into regular 1/16th notes as the line descends and shifts positions towards the A note on the 5th fret of the low E string in bar four. It can take a little time to get used to the *push and pull* of this study, but if care is taken to start each idea on its target beat, you can become accustomed to it. Play each portion at whatever rate of acceleration is required to get to the next on time.

Example 9h:

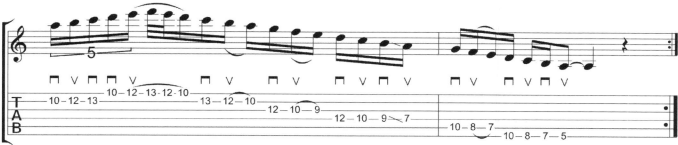

Chapter Ten: Studies in B Minor

Study 14 (Example 10a)

Ascending fours should feel like quite a fixture in your picking repertoire by now, which will be put to use in the B hybrid minor pattern in bars one, two and the first three beats of bar three. It leads to the discussion point of this study.

The pedal-point lick that extends from the 4th beat of bar three to the end of bar four is a point of focus in this example. Single pick strokes go back and forth between the high E string and B string without the pre-emptive hammer-on or pull-off that you have seen in descending and ascending fours sequences. As the 15th fret, high E string pedal-tone stays put, and the alternating notes travel down the B harmonic minor scale, consecutive outside-picked strokes are required when the lower notes move down to the B string in bar four.

Yngwie's picking motion for multi-string pedal-point always subtly incorporates the crosspicking approach discussed in connection with the lone note strategy, or the more mechanically-accurate description: wrist extension and flexion. Crosspicking was covered in Chapter Six, but for instances that require you to pick each note (like this example), there is only half the time to move the pick to either side of the string pair without any preparatory slur notes.

To build your crosspicking chops, take the four notes that occur in beat 2 of the fourth bar, and create a repeating drill from them. When later combined with the rest of Example 10a, your goal is to be able to pick the pedal-point element without any hindrance to the flow or tempo you establish in the first three measures.

Example 10a

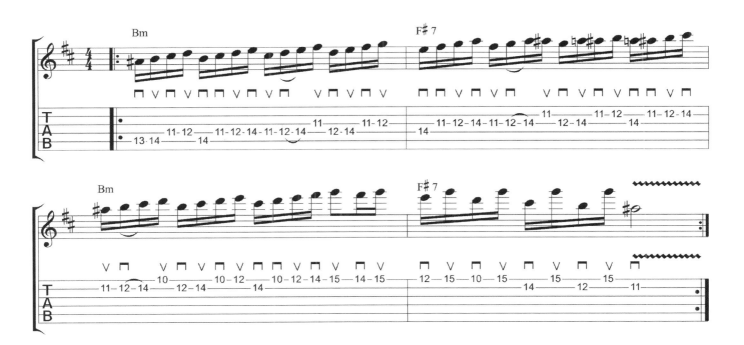

Study 15 (Example 10b)

Similar to the way the *Fives Turnaround* was used to switch positions after an even number (in an otherwise odd number of notes per string), the *Sevens Slide* adds a note to a group of six ascending notes via a slide at the end of the higher string in a pair.

In this study, an ascending B natural minor pattern in bar one has an extension slide on the high E string from the 12th fret to the 14th fret going to beat 4. This 14th fret F# note, while being a part of the Sevens Slide that began on beat 3, is also now the highest note in a new set of six beginning on the B string, 10th fret. Going into bar two of the example, the slide to the 15th fret of the E string is another occurrence of the Sevens Slide, so each time a slide occurs, the slid note becomes the sixth of a new group as the positions travel up the string pair.

Regarding notation, I have again interpreted Yngwie's tendency to rush the last four notes of bar one to allow the new position to begin in bar two. This rushing occurs in each instance of the Sevens Slide so that it need not take more time to play seven ascending notes than six would have. You can also experiment with playing each note with the same duration as the next, keeping in mind that as a result, you push back the sequence one 1/16th note for each occurrence of the Sevens Slide.

Example 10b:

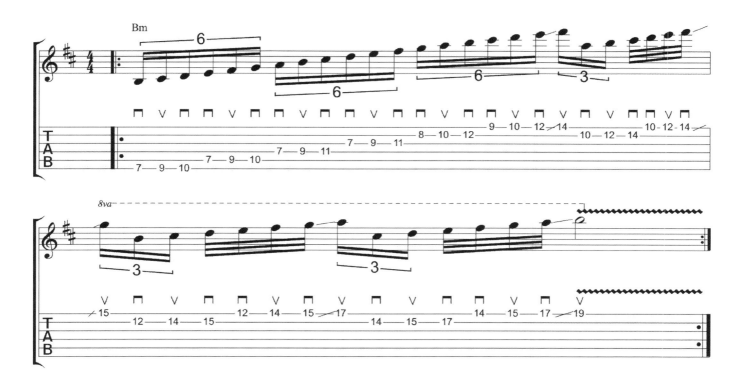

Study 16 (Example 10c)

The Sevens Slide can occur on other string pairs too, despite Yngwie's favouring of the B and high E strings. This natural minor scale example wanders up the A and D strings, beginning on the highest note in a six-string pattern, with slides occurring on the D string until the index finger arrives at the 7th fret of the A string. The B minor pattern from Example 10b is used to go from the fifth string to the first string, with a small legato burst occurring on the 2nd beat of bar two before returning to the B string to end the lick.

With all of the examples involving rushed-sounding timing, keep in mind that these speed bursts needn't be as stiff and precise as notated. One of the things that make Yngwie stand out as a creative and intuitive player is his knack for sounding a little loose even while executing some highly technical mechanics. Time feel is just as crucial in rock as it is in jazz, so find your groove as you develop this material.

Example 10c

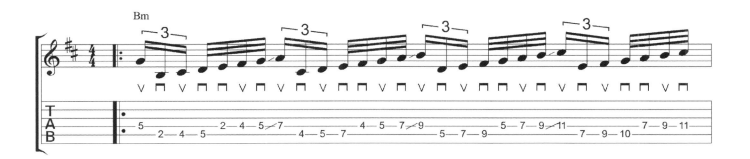

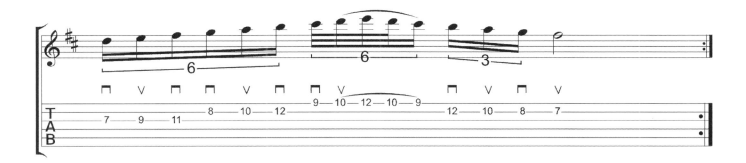

Study 17 (Example 10d)

The Switchblade is a name I gave to a descending position shift that I first noticed on Yngwie's *Live In Leningrad* concert on the track *Crystal Ball* back in 1989. The reason for the name was because of how quickly the high E string notes popped out from what would otherwise be a single-string descending fours sequence on the B string. This pattern occurs in bars one and two of Example 10d.

Relocating the first of each four-note group to a higher string has an intervallic appeal, but it also requires an upstroke on the higher string, and *down, up, down* on the lower string of a pair - a reversal of what would occur in descending fours on one string only. Crosspicking facilitates the transitions from the B string back to the high E string.

I have witnessed Yngwie playing this kind of pattern with a couple of different approaches over the years, but the one notated is the most technically consistent with his picking style. In situations where a more legato sound is desired, the upstroke on the E string and downstroke on the B string can be picked, and a pull-off and legato slide can initiate the remaining two notes of each four.

Example 10d

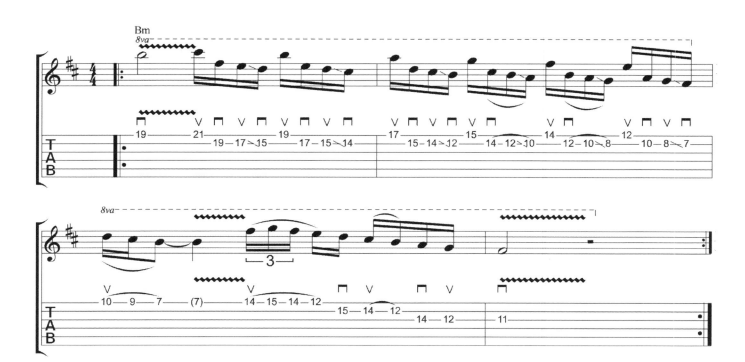

Study 18 (Example 10e)

For the last study piece, let's take Yngwie's version of crosspicking to its extreme with a lick that sandwiches it between two economy picking ideas using B harmonic minor. How Yngwie approaches sequences when his go-to system doesn't appear to fit, is one of the most common things I get asked. Riffs like *I Am A Viking* and *Anguish and Fear* raise questions because they challenge what we think we can or cannot do within the Yngwie system.

Two-string pedal-point licks have already shown us that playing the higher string on an upstroke and the lower string on a downstroke is the most *Yngwie* thing to do in the situation, so with the *thirds* descending sequence portion of Example 10e, it is a matter of applying that solution on a larger scale.

Cast your eyes to the third 1/16th note of beat 2, bar one. Here, the A# note on the 18th fret of the E string leads to the F# on the 19th fret of the B string using *up, down* pick strokes as per the pedal-point approach. The same applies to the next two notes. The rest of the descending sequence intersperses odds and evens as four notes per string are played *down, up, down, up,* and single notes occur with outside, alternating pick strokes. Doing so is, of course, alternate picking, but by leading with upstrokes, inside picking pathways are avoided and therefore as consistent with The Yng Way as possible. Spend some time on this portion of the study before adding the musical bookends on either side.

Leading into the thirds sequences is an ascending B minor (major VII) arpeggio on beat 1 of the first bar, executed with a sweep and one upstroke. The B and G notes that begin Beat 2 are, melodically speaking, the beginning of the thirds sequences downward, but are executed with a downstroke and a pull-off to set up the lone note upstroke on the 18th fret of the E string.

In bar two, a textbook economy-picked B harmonic minor pattern begins on the second 1/16th note of the 4th beat, which continues through bar three. At this point, you should raise one fist in the air and scream *I have mastered The Yng Way!*

Example 10e:

Conclusion

In my studies on this fantastic instrument, it has always been the concepts, motivations and systems behind things that have kept me picking up the guitar every day; to find the idea behind the ideas. So too, through your studies of this book and into the future, I hope that you enjoy the processes of understanding, working at, and applying its material to both Yngwie's music and your own.

From these pages, you have worked through a complex combination of strategies, which speaks to not only the genius of Yngwie Malmsteen's unique approach to the guitar but to your quest for knowledge and mastery. So, congratulations on getting this far!

This book is the kind that I expect that you'll need to re-read, backtrack and cross-reference multiple times, so I encourage you to do so, and not feel overly pressured to absorb everything on the first read through. I also urge you to use this book as a companion piece to Yngwie songs and solos you study or transcribe. Keep it close by and consult it anytime your intuition doesn't immediately provide a solution.

Some critics accuse Yngwie of being a repetitive player. I've always said that, rather than have a hundred tricks in his bag, Yngwie is a player who knows how to use five skills in twenty different ways each. As the concepts in this book manifest in your studies of the Malmsteen catalogue, they will become re-enforced through the very repetition that detractors would use to discredit his style.

In practice, divide your routine into portions just as the chapters in the book have. You won't likely have time to work on every lick every day but try to address your target areas of improvement with a selection of examples that focus on the relevant skill.

Play with gusto, and be relentless in your pursuits. That is The Yng Way!

Chris

Glossary of Terms

Active principle	A fundamental aspect of how motion will be carried out
Alternate picking	Picking that uses consistently opposing pick strokes, down and up
Anchoring	Placing of the picking hand on the guitar bridge
Anguish and Fear	Track 7 from the Yngwie Malmsteen album *Marching Out*
Anti-clockwise offset	Turning the pick anti-clockwise from the neutral position
Arpeggio	The notes of a chord, sounded individually either in rhythm or melody
Ascending fours	A scale sequence that moves upward in steps using four consecutive scale notes each time, e.g., A B C D, B C D E, C D E F etc
Auxiliary mechanics	Motions that occur because of or as a supplement to the primary function
Biomechanics	The laws relating to the study of movement and structure
Caprices, 24	A collection of compositions by Romantic-era violinist Niccolo Paganini
Clockwise offset	Turning the pick clockwise from the neutral position
Crosspicking	An alternate picking style that uses wrist flexion and extension to reposition the pick from string to string
Crotchet	A quarter note with a value of one beat in a 4/4 bar
Demisemi quaver	A thirty-second note with a value of an eighth of a beat in a 4/4 bar
Descending fours	A scale sequence that moves downwards in steps using four consecutive scale notes each time, e.g., A G F E, G F E D, F E D C etc
D-grip	Holding the pick in the shape of an uppercase D letter with the thumb and finger
Diatonic	Belonging to or derived from a key
Diminished 7th	An arpeggio consisting of degrees I, bIII, bV, bbVII
Downward pick slant	Tilting the back end of the pick downward so that downstrokes push in towards the guitar body
DPO	Downward picking orientation
Economy picking	Directional motion that results in a string starting with a continuation of the pick stroke that completed the previous string
Fireball	An album by the band Deep Purple
Fives Turnaround	A two-string pattern consisting of three notes on a string and two notes on a higher string, used to launch the fretting hand into another position

Forearm rotation	Picking hand motion that originates the from inwards and outwards movement of the forearm muscles rather than the wrist or elbow joints
Harmonic Minor Scale	A scale consisting of degrees I, II, bIII, IV, V, bVI, VII or natural minor with a major VII degree
Horizontal axis	In line with the guitar strings
Hybrid Minor Scale	A synthetic minor scale that includes both the bVII and VII degrees consecutively
Hybrid picking	Using the plectrum and picking hand fingers to pick notes
I am A Viking	Track 5 from the Yngwie Malmsteen album *Marching Out*
Imperfect Cadence	Harmonic tension created by concluding a passage with a I chord moving to a V chord in a major or minor key
Inside picking	A path along which the pick travels directly between the strings with the shortest distance
Lateral Tens	Ten-note melodic units moved sideways on a pair of strings
Legato	Tied together, smooth, consisting of hammer-ons and pull-offs
Lone note exception	The way of handling a single note on a string when other strategies do not apply
Natural Minor Scale	A scale consisting of degrees I, II, bIII, IV, V, bVI, bVII
Newtonian	Relating to the discoveries of Isaac Newton
Now Your Ships Are Burned	Track 3 from the Yngwie Malmsteen album *Rising Force*
NPS	An abbreviation of Notes Per String
Ostinato	A continually repeated phrase or rhythm
Outside picking	A path along which the pick travels the longest distance around the strings
Palm-muting	Using the picking hand to dull or silence the sound of strings
Parallel picking	Downstrokes and upstrokes that move parallel to the guitar body
Pedal-point	A melodic device in which a note is repeated while other notes alternately proceed without reference to it
Perfect Cadence	Harmonic resolution created by a V chord moving to a I chord in a major or minor key
Phrygian Dominant	A mode created from the notes of harmonic minor, arranged from the V degree and used over the V chord
Pick grip	Relating to how the hand and fingers position the guitar pick for playing

Pick orientation	The ongoing tendency to favour one kind of pick slant over the other
Pick edge offset	The state of having one edge of the pick positioned to contact the string first
Pick-gato	A portmanteau meaning to combine picking and slurs in a single phrase
Picking pathway	The route created by the motion of the pick
Pick slant	Leaning the pick forward or backwards along the vertical axis instead of at a 90-degree angle to the guitar body
Positional scale	A scale pattern that does not require sliding to more than one position
Pronation	Inward rotation of the forearm so that the surface of the hand faces downward
1/8th note	An eighth note with a value of half a beat in a 4/4 bar
Relative minor scale	The natural minor scale when referred to its formation from the VI degree of a major scale
Rest stroke	When the pick comes to a stop on a string before executing the next note
Rested principle	A fundamental aspect of preparing for motion in an optimum way
Semiquaver	A sixteenth note with a value of a quarter of a beat in a 4/4 bar
Sevens Slide	A two-string pattern consisting of three notes on one string and four notes on a higher string that includes a position shift
Slurs, slurring	Hammer-ons, pull-offs and legato-slides
Supination, active	Rotation of the forearm so that the surface of the hand faces outward
Supination, rested	A resting point already biased in favour of supination before motion has occurred
Supination bias	Downward picking orientation
Tapping	A two-handed technique using hammer-ons and pull-offs from fingers of the picking hand on the fretboard
Tonal Sequence	A melodic device in which a motif is repeated in a higher or lower pitch and subsequent repetitions are diatonic transpositions of the original idea
Tremolo picking	Picking the same note repeatedly at high speed
Triplet	Three notes played in the space that two of the same would typically occupy, e.g., a 1/8th note triplet played within the duration of two 1/8th notes
UPO	Upward picking orientation
Upward pick slant	Tilting the back end of the pick upward so that downstrokes move away from the guitar body

Vertical axis	Perpendicular to the guitar strings; parallel to the guitar body
Wrist deviation, radial	Sideways movement at the wrist joint towards the radius
Wrist deviation, ulnar	Sideways movement at the wrist joint towards the ulna
Wrist extension	Bending the wrist outwards from the neutral position
Wrist flexion	Bending at the wrist joint inwards from the neutral position
Yng Way, the	The state of playing within the principles contained in Yngwie's style

About the Author

Chris Brooks is a guitarist, educator and recording artist based in Sydney, Australia. What began as an obsession with '80s high octane lead guitar has, well, not changed at all.

A former student of the Australian Institute of Music, Brooks exhibited an early penchant for guitar-driven music, whether it was the sideman shredding of Kee Marcello and Brett Garsed, or the solo-artist career paths of Vinnie Moore, Steve Vai and Yngwie Malmsteen. The obligatory eight-hour practice sessions would be fuelled by lesson material from Hot Licks and REH videos as Brooks followed the trajectory to making his own guitar music and instructional content.

Releasing two solo albums, 2002's *The Master Plan* and 2011's *The Axis of All Things*, Chris has received acclaim from print and online media worldwide, including Japan where The Master Plan was included in *Young Guitar* magazine's *500 Essential Guitar Albums* special issue, and back home in Australia where *Australian Guitar* magazine rated him one of the top underground guitarists.

Brooks has also recorded with *Yngwie Malmsteen*'s former vocalist *Mark Boals*, Australian melodic metal band *LORD*, toured with major label band *Feeding the Addiction*, and appeared on compilation albums for labels including Frontiers (Europe), Marquee Inc. (Japan) and Liquid Note Records (UK).

As founder of **guitarlickstore.com**, Brooks has created popular guitar courses including *Sweep Picking Systems for Arpeggios*, *Picking Systems for Pentatonic*, and his most popular to date – *The Yng Way*, on which this book was based. Featuring nearly two hours of HD video, backing tracks, and PDF tablature and notation, The Yng Way has sold over 500 units and has been noted by many as a leading resource on the technique of Yngwie Malmsteen.

With a keen eye for the details of what makes things work on the guitar and an aversion to sleeping, Brooks is working towards a large body of educational resources and musical output.

32329431R00060

Made in the USA
San Bernardino, CA
13 April 2019